STREET PEOPLE SPEAK

STREET PEOPLE SPEAK
BY
RUTH MORRIS AND COLLEEN HEFFREN

MOSAIC PRESS
Oakville — New York — London

CANADIAN CATALOGUING IN PUBLICATION DATA

Morris, Ruth, 1933-
    Street people speak

ISBN 0-88962-364-3

1. Homeless persons - Ontario - Toronto.
I. Heffren, Colleen, 1951-   . II. Title.

HV4510.T67M67 1987   305.5'68'09713541
                     C87-094748-6

No part of this book may be reproduced or transmitted in any form, by any means, electronic or mechanical, including photocopying and recording information storage and retrieval systems, without permission in writing from the publisher, except by a reviewer who may quote brief passages in a review.

Published by MOSAIC PRESS, P.O. Box 1032, Oakville, Ontario, L6J 5E9, Canada. Offices and warehouse at 1252 Speers Road, Unit #1 & 2, Oakville, Ontario, L6L 5N9, Canada.

Mosaic Press acknowledges the assistance of the Canada Council and the Ontario Arts Council in support of its publishing programme.

Copyright © Ruth Morris and Colleen Heffren, 1988.
Design by Rita Vogel
Typeset by Aztext Electronic Publishing Ltd.
Cover illustration by Joe Fleming
Printed and bound in Canada.

ISBN 0-88962-364-3 PAPER

MOSAIC PRESS:
In Canada:
        MOSAIC PRESS, 1252 Speers Road, Units #1 & 2, Oakville, Ontario   L6J 5N9, Canada.

In the United States:
        Riverrun Press Inc., 1170 Broadway, Suite 807, New York, N.Y., 10001, U.S.A., distributed by Kampmann & Co., 9 East 40th Street, New York, N.Y., 10016

In the U.K.:
        John Calder (Publishers) Ltd., 18 Brewer Street, London, W1R 4A5, England.

TABLE OF CONTENTS

STREET PEOPLE SPEAK
Ruth Morris and Colleen Heffren

Acknowlegement	7
Introduction	9
Preface	13
CHAPTER ONE: OUR LIVES NOW	**15**
1. A day on the streets	15
2. Nights on the streets	20
3. Our health	22
4. Mental health	24
5. Our friends	26
6. Our children	31
CHAPTER TWO: WE BELIEVE	**39**
1. Best things in our lives	39
2. Worst things in our lives	41
3. Changing our ourselves	44
4. Dealing with depression	46
5. Our dreams: Three magic wishes	51
CHAPTER THREE: WHERE WE CAME FROM; BACKGROUND	**57**
1. How we got here	57
2. Our feelings toward family	67
3. Why we're on the street	73
CHAPTER FOUR: MEETING THE WORLD	**81**
1. School	81
2. Work	87
3. Agencies	90
4. How you see us	101

CHAPTER FIVE: OUR MESSAGE; TELL TORONTO THIS!	107
CHAPTER SIX: PROFILES	121
CHAPTER SEVEN: COMMUNITY ACTION	139
CONCLUSION	145
APPENDIX ON METHODOLOGY	149

ACKNOWLEDGEMENTS

This book would not have been possible without the generous and open sharing of all the homeless people we met, whose dignity deserves to be recognized.

The opinions in this book are entirely those of the authors and not of the Ministry of Housing which funded this project under their program for the 1987 U.N. Internatinal Year of Shelter For the Homeless. We appreciate the facilitiation of Ludovic de Sousa and Terry Fagan, and the support of The Honourable Alvin Curling, former Minister of Housing.

The assistance of all our volunteers was invaluable. Appreciation goes to Carmen Pratt, June Campbell, and Hugh Walkey, for assistance with interviewing; and Mark Trucz and Heinz Klein for donated time, skill and resources for obtaining

Ruth Morris and Colleen Heffren

the photographs. Most of the pictures were taken and donated by Mark Trucz whose expertise in photography and generosity gave the book its visual impact. David Langley donated more photos when he learned of this project.

We are particularly grateful for the cooperation of Ted Grizzel, Manager of Thrift Villa for support in facilitiating our gift certificates for the homeless.

This project would not have been complete without the information and shared experience of Michael Morrissette of the Red Door Shelter at Woodgreen Church; Rev. Brad Lennon of All Saints Church; John Jagt, Director of Metro's Hostels; STOP 103; Chris Watts; Ruth Crammond of St. Christopher's House; Michael Shapcott of Christian Resource Centre; Dave Walsh of Our Homes; and Dan Leckie of Councillor Jack Layton's office for Ward 6. The vision for so much of this came from the dreams and work of Rick Gordon and Rob Keehn.

INTRODUCTION

What could be more compelling than the knowledge that one-quarter of humanity endure the dire consequences of homelessness? That is, over 1,000 million people do not have adequate housing and of these approximately 100 million have no shelter whatsoever.[1] The contradiction of stark poverty juxtasposed against fantastic wealth is prevalent throughout the developed world: In the United States, there are about three million homeless, with fewer than 100,000 beds provided by the private sector.[2] While high-cost housing has replaced low-rent units, almost 50% of single room occupancy housing has been demolished. The same trend can be witnessed here in Canada, with the huge blight of homlessness growing across our Nation.

Ruth Morris and Colleen Heffren

The results of a snapshot survey by the Canadian Council on Social Development revealed that "during 1986, beds were provided to about 100,000 homeless and destitute people, and over one million meals were served by about 300 of Canada's shelters and soup kitchens."[3] These figures only hint at the magnitude of human suffering, since out of the 1,000 agencies contacted, less than half responded in time for inclusion in this survey. The stunning enormity of the numbers of Canadians seeking shelter can't help but cast a foreboding shadow over all of our lives.

The homeless in our midst are victims of our individualistic and achievment oriented society. Who are we to judge the "failure" of people who fall through the cracks and are forced to live deprived, barren lives, lacking in dignity, and hope? Who could survive with no chance of reclaiming their proper inheritance of fulfilled potential, without the bearing of a home. The "faitures" of the homeless, indeed, are so complex: they include the unemployed; underemployed; the disabled; the elderly; war veterans; abused women and children; ex-psychiatric patients; ex-convicts; alcoholics, and drug abusers; the anti-social; and the emotionally traumatized, who never found the needed support from family or friends. Rehabilitation of these varied and complex difficulties could be achieved with an outpouring of patience, love and willingness to support the vital healing processes. It is essential, however, to restructure communities to meet human needs and empower the most unempowered to regain control of their lives. It is also essential to dismantle the systemic policies which perpetrate poverty and homelessness.

The number one social and economic policy priority should be to improve employment opportunities and prevent the deterioration of existing jobs,[4] as well as planning for the development of large-scale low-cost housing; and policies to estalish adequate income. These economic imperatives must first be implemented to avoid negative impacts on all of society. We know that unemployment leads to violence, and often the homeless commit crimes. For some, prisons are a last resort to avoid freezing. The majority of prisoners in fact are the poor, who once institutionalized, become bitter, repeat offenders and often suffer damage beyond repair.

We, in the sheltered and safe world, tend to react with fear, sometimes with grief, and often with hositility to the spectre of destitute humans littering our streets and parks. We can't escape the haunting question lurking in our minds of how can so many people be reduced to such a state of irrecoverable destitution. It's easier to have them taken away and locked-up; out of sight, out of mind. Our attitudes towards the down-trodden as "degenerate, pathetic filth" are challenged in light of the exponential growth in homelessness itself. It is shocking how homelessness has spread to so many women, children, and middle class individuals, who are now caught in the jaws of poverty. The vulnerability of the middle class is evident when we consider that more than four million Canadians, that is one in six, live below the poverty line. This further translates into at least one million Canadians who are without shelter, or live in inadequate housing.[5]

Children are the hardest hit by the reality of unequal economic opportunity. The child Poverty Action Group in Toronto warn us that "In 1985, more than 1.1 million children - one out of every five - were living in poverty in Canada. In Ontario alone, an estimated 330,000 children under eighteen years of age are experiencing the economic, social, and educational barriers that come with being poor.[6] If the children of today are failed and not nourished with the emotional and economic support of a stable home life, the structure of our future society will be undermined.
Our collective social responsibility to children is evident, particularly as it is declared that "the national neglect of children is rooted in a cultural and political bias against families raising children."[7] The unemployment status of the parents directly affects child poverty and tends towards the present "feminization" of poverty, with over-representation of women among Canada's poor. In 1961, only 13.2% of poor families were headed by women; but in 1985, this had climbed to 36.5%[8]

In this book, we bring you the tragic tales of the "unsuccessful" members of our production-consumer society. Their compelling struggles for self-worth and dignity, in search of mere subsistence, employment, shelter, food and friendship, are awesome. Each of us needs to be aroused and to demand the end to the dehumanizing and socially destabilizing conditions of widespread poverty. If the plight of the poor continues to be ignored, the foundation of our democratic and future society is in jeopardy. As a responsible society, we owe the destitute the humane chance of a home and an adequate income, as this is crucial to the stability of any human being. The perpetration of poverty is a crime against humanity which should no longer be tolerated, especially in our wealthy overdeveloped societies.

FOOTNOTES

1. United Nations Statistics *Canadian Housing* Vol. 3, No.2 p.145.

2. Ibid, p.25.

3. *Social Development Overview* Vol.4, No.3, CCSD 1987.

4. Ibid., Vol.4, No.1, 1986, p.8.

5. *Canadian Housing,* Vol.4, No.1, The Canadian Association of Housing and Renewal Officials, 1987.

6. *National Income Programe for Children, Polocies to End Child Poverty,* Child Poverty Action Group, 1987.

7. Ibid.

8. *Social Infopac,* Vol.5, No.4, Social Planning Council of Metropolitan Toronto, December 1986.

Rita Vogel

PREFACE

We all have fleeting encounters with street people, but rarely do we have the time or the courage to find out who they are. We rarely share with them anything in the much needed level of human caring. The experience of walking up and talking to strangers who are shabbily dressed and often distraught is profoundly moving. While many people we approached were open and willing to share their stories, others would react with fear and try to get away as fast as possible. Their worlds are so fragile and insecure. They don't trust anyone and it is much safer to avoid contact with people on the "outside". Indeed, living on the streets is very dangerous and many remarked that is "safer" to keep to themselves, and "not to make too many friends". However, under the sometimes hardened exterior, we found the homeless to be articulate, open, humble, and often very shy.

It is frightening to see the growing numbers of homeless people. Perhaps it is our fear which makes it easier to "blame the victim" than to recognize the systemic conditions which perpeterate homelessness. The problems of inadequate income, unemployment and lack of affordable housing, combine to crush the innocent, even those in the middle class who least expect to join the ranks of homeless.

Ruth Morris and Colleen Heffren

Many myths prevail about the homeless, such as: "these people choose to be there - they just don't want to work - drunks deserve their lot." Not all street people are drunks, they are not all lazy bums, and they are not all criminal, though they are often forced to become this way. Many are fathers and mothers whose marriages failed. Many are still children, who are deprived the chances of childhood; manyhave physical and psychological disabilities. Many become drunks because this is the only way to cope with their profound despair. These downtrodden people are also remarkably caring, sensitive and courageous, gentle souls. Denied access to housing and survival resources, ultimately they just fall through the cracks, and lose their ability to get out again.

STREET PEOPLE SPEAK is a testimony to the life threatening reality of low-income, unemployment and the lack of affordable housing. The bureaucratic band-aid barricades built around the poor are not working, because of these systemic economic conditions which perpetrate poverty and homelessness. Toronto's social service system, reputedly one of the best in Canada, is barely working. No one is free from the threat of homelessness and all the consequent physical, psychological and social scars which the homeless suffer. As a society, we pay a price for the clutter of institutionalism which is not designed to meet human needs, nor to solve the systemic conditions which trap the vulnerable in our society.

Each person we spoke with is unforgettable, even the ones who turned bitterly away, saying they weren't interested. They sometimes are the most haunting of all. We don't know the grief and indignity of pounding the concrete day after day, with very little hope to sustain them. The voices of this silent society come to life in this book to teach us and to arouse us to see their world as it is. This world of human neglect and misunderstanding raises very important questions about ourselves and the society we bequeath to the future.

CHAPTER ONE: OUR LIVES NOW

1. A Day on the Streets

"Every morning I walk and walk, trying to bum money. Doing anything I can. Finally just crying, it is so depressing. I wouldn't recommend it for anybody."

Those of us who have always had a warm home to go back to cannot imagine how street people spend the hours, day or night, when there is nowhere to go back to, no cozy hobby spot, no place to be when you are sick or well, day or night.

It makes some difference whether your are drinking or sober; spending nights on the street itself or in some kind of hostel; young or old. A few of the native alcoholics gave us clear accounts of their routines. Tim described it this way:

15

"My friends and I stand one another, encourage each other to drink. This is a rough town. We meet each other in the morning if we didn't sleep together. After we have a bite at Scott or at Caring Corner we head down Bloor Street, three guys stemming (begging) together. When we get enough for a couple of jars of wine, we sit by the tracks on Dupont, drink some. Then we stem on the way back, get enough for four to five jugs. We sit back and relax, alternating stemming and drinking with friends, three or four of us together."

Anyone imagining this to be an idyllic life enjoyed at our expense should have seen the ugly wounds on his head or heard the despair in his voice hidden behind the thin veneer of bravado. Isaac, another native person, described the pattern many street people have of browsing for bottles to pick up and sell. Otherwise, he spends his day sitting in the park. Young Jerry described the volatile irregularity of youth on the street:

"I don't have a regular schedule; sometimes I stay awake for days, then sleep for a day. But when I do have a normal kind of day, I wake up, and if I have money, get a coffee. I panhandle. I see friends, and try to get money together for a meal, for alcohol and drugs, but I don't do any heavy drugs. I get food at Stop 103, and the Scott Mission. If I'm real hungry and can afford it I get a slice of pizza."

Tom describes the life of a man with a drinking problem who has spent 5 long years on the street, day and night:

"I wake up early, go to the Scott Mission, and hang around the side hoping for work. People come by with trucks or phone in sometimes, who want cheap labour. If there is no work, I stay there for a meal. Around noon, I take a walk downtown, and browse; the odd time I go down to Harbourfront. I roam around all day like a lost soul, always looking for work all day. If I see a truck unloading I'll ask, 'Do you need a hand.'

STREET PEOPLE SPEAK

In the evening I tend to go the Soctt till 10 p.m., drinking coffee, watching TV. Then I go looking for a place to sleep, usually a drop box."

Another man with a drinking problem who had spent years on the street described his routine in even more graphic detail:

"After walking the streets at night when it is cold, and alternating that with lying on the street vents, I start the day at 5. By 5:30 I am eating hamburgers stolen from MacDonald's garbage, for my breakfast. I pick up cigarette butts til 7:30. At 7:30, I go to the Caring Corner, and sit there by myself. After that I try for work with small businesses I know, approaching contacts. If I get work, it lasts six hours till 5, and I get $30. Most of the time, I drink it, and that night and next day am hungover and won't go to work. Then it takes two to three days to get my health back again so I can work again. When I don't drink, I try for a steady job, walk the streets, sometimes read, vegetate, lie down somewhere, lie on benches, pick up butts, and read short stories I take from dropins. I prefer to steal them; it gives me a sense I can do SOMETHING."

Those not as addicted to alcohol, but who still sleep on the streets have their patterns too. A common problem is how to keep warm in cold wet weather. Person after person speaks of the wretchedness of the numbing cold and of always being so tired. You never can sleep properly in the cold winter nights on the street. They say the cold is an affliction, day and night:

"So cold. I would walk to keep warm, sit in the park from weariness, then walk some more to get warm. I did it one solid week, and if I had it to do over again, I would kill myself. I tried staying with a friend, but I ended up totally his maid. Finally I tried to get on welfare, but I didn't know anything about them..."

Others describe the endless search for rooms and jobs, with no phone to use and no phone to be called at.

Paul sleeps on empty trains at Union Station. He has a somewhat more cheerful routine:

"I wake up in the morning on the train, go to stores and say I lost money in their machines. They usually give me a little money. Then I walk around Yonge Street, hoping to find something somewhere, food or money, asking people sometimes. Then I come to this drop-in and make calls about jobs. If I don't get day work, I go for more money or food in the afternoon. I hang around till 10 or 11, and then head for the trains and go to sleep. Mostly I eat peanuts and pop, but I have one meal at the drop-in."

The eternal round of activity to keep alive is as evident in their lives as in ours. Only most have to work without any of the breaks we enjoy in order to get the minimum requirements for continued existence. Donald describes his lonely existence: "I wake up on the street at 6, try for morning coffee. I buy it if I have money, otherwise get it at a dropin or am sometimes given a cup. I try for a paper, pick one up someone has left. Usually the Star or Sun have better ads. I read all the job ads in my field; if I find one I might fit, I go and leave my application. I usually try for an interview. I get secondhand stuff for meals; stale muffins, etc. I read the paper from cover to cover, sitting on a bench. Sometimes if it is warm enough in the day, I nap for a couple of hours."

Those who usually sleep in hostels often have a more structured routine. They have a longer and better night's sleep, notwithstanding all the limits of hostels. A young unemployed man with minimal work history is proud of having taught himself to play the piano. He played it at a community centre, as an important part of his routine. He also exercises and goes to the library. Brent, a bright young man, describes his days:

STREET PEOPLE SPEAK

"If I sleep in a hostel, I wake up at 6:30 - if I want breakfast, at 5. Breakfast is 5:30 and 6:30 at Seaton. There is one wakeup call for it and if you don't hear, too bad. We have to be out by 7 a.m. I go to this centre by 7:30 - it's open nice and early, so I sit in the lobby and read a book or nap. Then I go to the drop-in and play a couple of games, scrabble or bridge, then to CRC for lunch. After that the afternoon at All Saints. Check in at Seaton at 4, supper at 5 or 6, watch TV there, go to bed. Whether I sleep or not at night depends on the drunks."

Jeff, whose sense of humor was still surviving his relatively short stay on the street, described his day this way:

"Out of the hostel by 7 a.m. Walk to Caring Corner for coffee; then to Scott for 10 a.m. meal if the weather is bad, then stay for the 11 a.m. meal if I don't expect other meals that day. If the weather is good, go to Union Station, and watch the lucky people go to work, while I read the Sun.

If it's cold, go to Eaton's Centre and underground places. If it's a nice day, sit in the parks. If I have $3, I can to to the Island to avoid bottles of bitters, or having some drunk fall over you. Or look at store windows, look, because you can't buy anything. You fantasize about what you would buy if you ever have money again.

Every other day, you make it to O'Neill's Bathhouse on George Street, beside Seaton, to have a shower. You just want to escape the area.

Around 3, you can go to Good Shepherd for their 4:00 meal; it uses time and saves money to walk. Then if you have a meal ticket, you can go to Sally Ann. If you know your way around the street, it is impossible to starve, but it's very hard to find a bed, or clean clothes.

By 7 you go to the Scott for TV and to read the Star. Seaton is really bad with bitters at the end of the month. By 9, you are in bed and talk with a buddy awhile. It's hard to get even the temporary work, cause the bitters boys will work for less. Besides, the temporary services pocket half your wage from the employer, and that galls you."

The older rooming house crowd are not strictly speaking on the street, but on the edge of it. They have their own routine, going from dropins to seniors clubs, picking up bottles for small cash to stretch their very limited pensions. But days on the street are greatly affected by how you spend your nights.

2. Nights on the Streets

People sleep on the street in an incredible variety of places. Many are ingenious or just plain unlikely: alleyways, parks, under verandas, in unlocked cars, abandoned houses, stairwells, garages. Most homeless people have some variety, finding slightly warmer options in the winter. One person reported using apartment building hallways in cold weather, or the nursing station of an apartment building. Others call on friends if possible in the winter's worst weather, but few have this option. More use hostels more in the winter, though reluctantly.

One thirty-three year old alcoholic avoids hostels because of the noisy young people. Another, a younger street person, complained that whether he slept at night or not depended on the drunks. When one thinks about it, however, there is no more reason to think that street people should enjoy the togetherness of hostel living than suburban dwellers would were they forced to sleep together.

Bob, a pro with fifteen years on the street, describes his efforts to survive the nights:

"My first ten years I slept mainly in hostels in winter, but now I use heating vents in winter, or coffee shops, or just walk the streets all night. I wear two pairs of pants, sweaters, and coats, but am still so cold I never really sleep. I'm semi-conscious all the time. Terrible, unceasing weariness.

STREET PEOPLE SPEAK

Another man described how he spent winters working at travelling carnivals in order to escape the bitter nights. He also tried under bridges, between warehouses and backyards, but all of these left him vulnerable to the weather. An older man while working for someone slept in an unheated garage until he could not take the cold anymore. Tim, a native alcoholic, describes another danger:

> "You got to stick together at nights on the street to avoid getting knifed. Anything can happen if you sleep alone. There is always one guy watching out for the group."

Finally, Tom, a veteran of many years on the street, day and night, describes his night survival techniques:

> "I sleep in stairwells, drop boxes, and once spent a whole winter in an abandoned house. I use hostels when I'm tired of old, dirty clothes, just to get cleaned up and a good meal and a good night's sleep for a change. In winter, I climb inside a drop box, and pull clothes over me for warmth.
>
> Sure it scares people who collect sometimes, but most who work for Goodwill or the Sally Ann have been on the street themselves, so they don't get mad. Rainy days, there's nowhere to go - you go in the shopping malls and the security guys kick you out in the rain.
>
> Sometimes it is hard to get out of the boxes. I caught my foot once for two minutes. When you want to get out, you have to peek out first. If you see two police cars, you wait till they take off. You have to watch that noone sees you getting in or out. Once I was sleeping in a bin full of rugs, and I woke up with smoke all around me. I went leaping out and scared the heck out of the security guys. They tried to charge me with starting it, but even the police could see it didn't make sense I would set a fire and go to sleep on it. By that time it was 5 a.m. and the police asked me where I would spend the rest of the night, as my clothes were soaked from the water they had used on the

flames. I said I guessed I would just walk around, so they invited me to ride in their car to keep warm till my clothes dried."

There is a mixed saga of near tragedy, humour and compassion in nights on the street. Days on the street can be lonely and weary, but nights of dark and cold have a special, endless quality of despair.

3. Our Health

About a third of the people we talked with reported no health problems. Whether this is a function of their realitve youth, or the fact that street people have to learn to ignore a lot of personal discomfort is hard to determine. Certainly, some of those who denied health problems were middle aged alcoholics who obviously had problems.

The health problems most often identified were: problems with legs, heart, teeth, back, lungs, mental health, eyes, and arthritis. Slightly smaller numbers reported difficulties with epiliepsy, their hands, acne, and hypertension. Of those who identified problems, about a third were getting help, a third were getting no help, and a third gave mixed replies, some help but not altogether satisfactory. A wide variety of reasons were given for not getting help. Stan, an older man, was reluctant to ask:

"I have some arthritis, not too serious, and my teeth need fixing. I should ask for welfare, but I never have."

Some fear hospitals. One chronically institutionalized man didn't want to see the inside of one at any cost:

"I have bronchitis and asthma. I don't want medical treatment - what could they do for me. Even when I broke my leg, I wouldn't go to hospital. They might keep me for two years, and I need freedom."

STREET PEOPLE SPEAK

The most common reason given for not seeking treatment was a feeling that medical services didn't see the homeless as human beings worthy of service:

> "I get blackouts, my mind is slipping. As for the bashes I get when I am drunk, I never seek treatment for them. They would just stitch me up and send me out. They know if you are a drunk you are in and out: they want you to give up and die."

> I got asthma, epilepsy and a leg infection. Doctors won't help me because when they look at my leg, they won't touch me, and just tell me to go away."

> "My sinuses don't drain properly and I need an operation. The doctors don't think it necessary, but they don't have to live with it. The clinic set up at SPACE was very good quality; it was in touch with the people here, and it didn't look down on people like doctors do, which is why many people here won't go. It is first come first served at the clinic."

In spite of these complaints, there were fewer criticisms of health sevices than we had anticipated. People live with their disabilities. One man commented sadly on his poor health and explained the reasons for being on the street:

> "I'm fifty-six years old, and worked for decades. Six years ago, I went on a moving job for Help Unlimited (irony unintended). After two hours, I lifted a heavy weight and my back gave out. My heavy working days were over, and I've never been able to do much work since."

We asked about eating habits. It is glaringly obvious that it is difficult to get a balanced diet and good nutrition on the street, although there have been some heroic contributions by some places to supply good meals.

The group that stood out the most for health problems were the natives. Most of them had multiple, serious problems and few were not getting any medical help at all:

> "Had asthma since birth. I have dental problems, 10% vision, and a hole in the heart. I see a doctor once a month."

> "Dental problems, only one eye, heart problems, bad kidneys, bad legs. I don't see a doctor - I don't like them."

> "I have arthritis, bronchitis, dental problems, a sore hip, bad legs, a curved back, and an injured hand. No, I wouldn't go to a doctor."

> "I'm deaf in one ear from sandblasting, have back problems, and leg problems. No, I don't get medical care."

Tim probably expressed best the alienation of the alcoholic natives from health care:

> "I'm hyper and quick tempered. The only treatment is bitters."

4. Mental Health

A more alarming problem is the number of severely mentally ill persons we interviewed. Here are samples from a few of the interviews.

> Jim, a native with echophalia, tended to repeat phrases over and over. In answer to our question about life on the street, he began with the score of the previous night's hockey game and went on:

> "Detroit Redwings 3 - 0. I don't swear, peanutbutter with, peanutbutter with...

> Best thing, let's see, I like sex, lovely sex (giggles), let's see, let's see, let's see, let's see..."

> School: "You won't believe it, I'm a doctor."

STREET PEOPLE SPEAK

Work: "There's a big crowd recording, recording, recording.."

Agencies: (giggle) "Let's see, let's see, let's see, how about opening this place up Saturdays and Sundays, have your own spaghetti - spaghetti and meatballs, I like spaghetti and meatballs. How 'bout rigatoni?"

The rest of the interview was a medley of all these themes - "the Detroit Redwings, lovely sex, spaghetti, and let's see, let's see" - dished up randomly between giggles. What had led him to the street?:

"Somebody threw me in the machine. I went nuts for six months, slow disintegration. Somebody threw a bomb, and I flew around."

The interviewer comments:

"At this point, I took him for a coffee and donut, and he started to relax and explain himself a little better!"

This kind of heroism in the field may sound funny. But it was very sad to see these lost souls wandering around, to touch them briefly, and then walk off and leave them to the terrifying challenges of street life. One interview truly was frightening:

"I think of going to the bridge and jumping off. Or going to the U.S. getting a gun and shooting someone, then killing myself. The TTC rode over my basketball when some punks were beating me up, and no one will take responsibility. I want to get even with all the people who have screwed me. I want justice. I'd like to meet a blind girl and cut off her breast, just like me...There's a constant stream of noise, I go insane with it..."

It is a terrifying thought that this walking time bomb, seething with inner pain and violence, is left to wander our streets untreated and subject to all the infinite provocations of life on the streets. We did our best to make referrals for anyone we thought we could help. But it takes more than a couple of well-intended interviewers working on a book to begin to heal this kind of pain and the serious mental illness on the street!

5. Our Friends

One of the redeeming aspects of every human situation is the tendency of human beings to support one another in the direst circumstances. I remember a speaker from India commenting on how the poor, having nothing else to give one another, huddle together on the strets of India to share their bodily warmth. Alas, we have seen this in Toronto, too.

Many of those we interviewed are loners, too hurt by rejection to link up, even to their fellow sufferers:

> "I have no friends. I hide in solitude while I wait till life brings a better side. Then I might have something to share, and would make friends in the process."

Walt also expresses the feeling that you must have something to give in order to gain friends:

> "When a person loses their job, you only feel better when you get another one. You have to try and try and try and try. When you're without a job, you don't hope no more; you stay in your room and sit in the park. It's lonely - it's not nice. You can't buy things you are supposed to buy; you read the paper a lot for jobs and news. I have friends, but can't depend on them. My friends are in the same situation. If you have money, you have friends; no money, no friends. You can't do anything without money."

What Walt really seems to be saying is that the thing he needs most is a job. Unfortunately, neither he nor his jobless friends can solve this problem for each other. Other loners expressed their fears of relating closely:

"I don't trust anybody too much. I don't show my feelings, just try to be as pleasant as possible."

"I have acquaintances, but no one very close. I don't let anyone get very close, but it does feel lonely most of the time."

"A few, but most people I know have gone away, been busted, or died. Most have been in jail or been vagabonds."

"No, basically I am a loner. Friends would hold you back from what you want to do..."

Beyond the loners, a considerable group of street people, mostly the alcoholics, have "drinking buddy" kinds of friends:

"Many, many friends. I don't see my brother often, and he is also an alcoholic, but we feel close. He listens to my problems. Another drinking buddy has gone to jail with me, and we spent a long time on the street together. We get emotional support from one another."

A moving example of friendship arose during one interview I did on a park bench. Throughout my interview with Tim, his friend Denny kept falling over the bench, then trying to get up, and collapsing onto the cement. Tim would always catch him before he could land and place him gently back on the bench. When Denny first got up to go, I said goodbye rather cheerfully, as I found his tendencies to collapse onto me or onto the cement equally distraacting. But Tim corrected me emphatically:

"Oh no, when he goes, I go!"

After that I joined in the efforts to keep Denny happy and upright. Tim described their friendship in this way:

"My friend here is on the same road as me. We've been drinking together since Christmas - that's five months!

He's my best friend. He understands me - we communciate. If I don't see him for two or three days, he looks for me. We check out places, and sooner or later, we see each other at the Scott or somewhere. We talk and sing together."

The native friend we visited in jail was feeling a little disillusioned with the fact that his drinking friends weren't able to visit him in jail. He observed:

"They're not really friends, just a bunch who follow you round, chipping together to get bottles of wine or bitters. When you're in trouble they don't see you, just friends when you're outside.

But when I was outside, we would talk about working, in the mornings on the street. Sometimes you're the banker. Someone gets his check, calls the boys and says, 'Don't worry about drinks today - I'm getting my check.'

A few of my friend are dead already: drunk or frozen in the street."

Tom, whose years of drinking and struggling against drinking on the street had left him very sensitive observed:

"I have lots of friends, all alcoholics. I have a few real good friends. Sometimes I get depressed when they get beat up. They are always in and out of the hospital. It hurts me inside because they are too drunk to take care of themselves. I can see that within them they are looking for help, but they don't have the power to use it. They have a lot of pride: they want to do it themselves. They are looking for you to help them, and you can't. You see intelligent people there who have held jobs, but something happened and they turned to the bottle - just like me; I couldn't face my divorce."

STREET PEOPLE SPEAK

The stark contrasts of the luxurious dressing of downtown department store manequins against the empty lonely shell of Toronto's street people brings home the absurdity of neglecting human needs.

Ruth Morris and Colleen Heffren

An impoverished and lonely eldery man who usually finds relaxation at Toronto's All Saints Church where he enjoys sharing war tales.

Tom has so much insight for others. He is working now to apply it to his own life. One can only hope and pray he will succeed.

The largest group of comments involved friendship beyond drinking, the bonds of fellowship in adversity and real mutual understanding. As Tar put it:

"My friends are people in the same boat as me."

Brent describes the bonds this way:

"Most of my friends have been down, or are in the process of getting out of it: friends on the streets and friends through my hobbies, mostly my age. These guys aren't going to let down on you. It's just being there, knowing you are not alone. There's also a special support from people getting out: if they can do it, you can too."

Some commented on the value of being able to give to others through friendship:

"I sometimes spend a night in a doughnut shop with someone giving them support. They know I am on the street, so they accept me more: I'm on the same level. The best way to help people on the street is to BE on the street."

"Most of my friends are on welfare, FBA... We see each other go up and down like yoyos. We support each other mentally: 'Don't give up, keep up the good work.'"

Jerry described the fellowship of punk rockers:

"Punk rockers are like a family. The woman I am staying with is crazy, literally, and she doesn't have anything but this apartment for a few months. So she has opened it up to anyone who needs a place, and all she asks is that you keep it quiet from 1 to 6 a.m., and respect her things. I heard about her through another friend."

Ruth Morris and Colleen Heffren

Street people help one another in the same way middle class people do, such as in the search for jobs and homes. It is just that they have fewer resources to share and the resources they do have are on a lower level. One commented:

> "I use friends more than anything in the job and room search."

Jim has learned a lot from his experience on the street and from the friends he has made there:

> "I have all kinds of friends, and no one type: some of the bitters boys too. Most street people are taking care of other street people. There is camaraderie: everyone helps everyone else. There is also our own justice system. I have seen people open a fresh pack and not share; later others will refuse them.
>
> But you appreciate support more than ever before. It shows me it can happen to anyone. It changes your thinking: not everyone on the street is a bitters boy. There are a lot of intelligent and good people, and the SYSTEM IS TRYING TO MAKE THEM INTO BITTERS BOYS."

Andre described the fellowship among homeless families. Because of the overflow in the family hostel these families are housed in a cheap motel by the city:

> "There is a family feeling in this motel. Many of the families are in this fix, and everyone is helping one another. We keep to ourselves in some ways, but still have good friends, because that is all we do have.
>
> I met a young girl here who helps in maintenance. Her stepfather molested her sister - the police didn't do anything, and their mother preferred him, so now the girls are struggling to make it on their own. People are very supportive of her."

Andre also told a moving story of the friendship they had received from a female taxi driver:

> "When my wife was ready to come out of the hospital with the baby, we had to have a car seat or they wouldn't let her out. This taxi driver when she learned of it, not only went out and bought a brand new carseat for the baby, but a whole set of things for her. Since then she has bought milk for the baby, and visited us. She finally told us what helped her understand so fully: her son had beaten her up, and she was feeling deeply what it meant to bring a child into this world. So she turned that terrible experience around and made it reach out to help us and give us back some faith and hope in our trouble."

Andre and his wife felt a profound gratitude for this touching gesture. There was no doubt that this woman's love had affected them in their darkest times. But Andre was also honest enough to see his own limitations. He commented that he found it hard to relate to some of his former friends because, even though their intentions were good, he had trouble not resenting their affluence in the face of his plight.

5. Our Children

Many of the isolated men we talked with are the fathers from broken homes. One of the sad things we learned is that there are not two, but three tragedies in these families. Behind the economically deprived single mother trying to support children who are deprived of both financial and emotional security, there is often a father. Broken and even more lonely, he sometimes ends up on the street. This does not justify any side of the case, but it is a grim reminder that everyone suffers in these situations.

The street people we interviewed are disproportionately single. Sixty percent have never married, not even common law, even though the average age is about thirty-three. Most of the remaining ones do have at least one child. And the vast majority of these have from one to three children. Outside of the hostel parents who were seeing their children daily, only two parents (7% of all the parents) were seeing them weekly. The rest had only occasional contact or none at all. Indeed, the majority who were not living with their children had no contact.

This void is one of the poignant things in their lives. Len, a native whose wife and four children are separated from him, says:

> "I worry about my children, because I don't get to see them. I feel great rage at being separated from them, because they are the only positive things in my life. I see them every three months. My own mother cries about it every time she sees me."

Of those who have been married, about half never see their spouse. This is another aspect of the total separation from family. Lee, a native who lived in common law, never sees his spouse and had three children, one of whom is dead. He rarely sees the other two. Another native reported that he didn't know if one of his children was dead.

Stan is a gentle older man with a drinking problem. When we asked him about his grown son who has written him off and won't see him since he hit the streets, he responded:

> "My son doesn't like his children calling me Grandpa in public. I have a daughter I haven't seen in ten years, from five till fifteen. I wonder about her, but her mother wouldn't let me see her."

Tom, who blamed only his drinking for the breakup of his marriage, told a particularly heart-rending story of his separation from his daughter:

> "The lowest point for me was when my daughter was five, about a year after our marriage breakup. I was seeing my daughter on the weekends, and she felt so close to me that she would cry and be upset for a couple of days after I

returned her. So one day my wife called and said it wasn't good for her, it upset her too much, so I shouldn't see her anymore. That year I got over $1,000 in drunk fines. Two months after that decision, I tried suicide, when I thought too much about my daughter, and missing her. It took me about a year to begin to get used to the pain."

A considerably brighter picture, but still one full of stress, comes from families or single parents living with their children in hostels. The growing problem of homeless families is having a massive impact on cities in both Canada and the USA. In an article in the *American Psychological Association's Monitor*, entitled "Homeless Families", (April, 1987 Susan Landers reports that a recent national survey indicates 30% of America's homeless are families with children. In Philadelphia, nearly half the people in its shelters were families and New York City's number of homeless families in shelters has increased in five years from 700 to 5,000. The director of Toronto's family hostel reports a dramatic increase also in the past three years in homeless families here. She observed:

"There are 50 to 175 homeless CHILDREN here at any one time. Their families have often been trailing around the country, trying to find a place and a job. And even if their parents have not always made the best decisions, why should these children have to suffer so much?"

One single mother in a hostel put it:

"Being homeless hurts. It's hard on the kids."

Another commented on the conditions that drove her to the hostel:

"The old house we rented was sold, and we had no money for first and last month's rent for a new place. Then we had three small children. It's O.K. to have dogs and cats in this world, but NOT KIDS."

Another young mother spoke of both the joy and the sorrow of parenting under such stressful conditions:

Ruth Morris and Colleen Heffren

"Sometimes it's so hard, because last year we had so much. My daughter says, 'Mommy, don't worry about it, cause when we grow up, we are gonna help you.' It's hard not being in control of my life."

The same mother described her struggle to use her strength to protect her child:

"I write poetry for myself. I cry on my own. I sleep in the same bed with my daughter, so I try not to cry with her there. When I am down, I think 'Better days will come. You are not crippled: you will be much stronger.' I feel my own strength."

Two parents I interviewed in a tiny hostel-rented motel room demonstrated gentle, beautiful parenting throughout the interview. Each child's needs were met quietly and lovingly. Their two year old brought in a bug, with all the pride of naive childhood. The mother quietly pointed out the exquisite wings and gave him pride in his discovery. All this was done without interfering with our talk, but in a way that showed respect for the child and no squeamishess at his wonderful discovery.

A father expressed his devotion to his family and new baby, in spite of the stress and distress of their setting.

"I had an apartment and furnishings and all kinds of good things, but I never had a FAMILY before. I have never experienced this sort of joy. Even in the midst of all we are suffering, it is such a joy. It certainly takes my mind off of immediate problems. I'm even more worried how the baby will make the transition to more space and less intimacy when we can find a proper home. The first thing she does when she wakes in the morning is look around for me!"

Tenderness for children is no monopoly of the housed. The grief of a lost family and lost children often played a significant part in sending people to the street. Their yearning for their lost children is expressed by Rob Keehn, a man who fell

STREET PEOPLE SPEAK

into the street when he lost his wife and family, and whose songs come from the soul of the street people's suffering:

SUNDAY FATHERS - SUNDAY FOOLS

1. *You can see us every weekend at the parks and hot dog stands*
   And the kids in matching baseball hats are clinging to their hands;
   We're doin' all those fun things, basking in those tiny smiles,
   And the time we have is far too short, and lasts for too few miles.

CHORUS:

> *Oh, it's tough to be a daddy, when your children live away,*
> *Cause you miss the joys and sorrows they live through every day;*
> *So you grit your teeth and bear it, living by those lawyers rules,*
> *An you'll see us in the park each week, Sunday fathers, Sunday fools.*

2. *So in quiet desparation, we do the most we can,*
   Cause it's lonely through the weekdays for a displaced family man
   And the thing that keeps us going is the ending of the week,
   And the laughter of our children is the only joy we seek.

   (CHORUS)

3. *Y'see we're the good time charlies who buy candy and ice cream*
   And 'cause the time we have's too short, we try to answer dreams
   Oh, we can't say no 'cause the smiles we get have to feed us seven days,
   Y'see it's not just kids who suffer 'cause we've gone our separate ways.

Ruth Morris and Colleen Heffren

(CHORUS)
Rob's own experience is expressed more closely still in his song about his own little girl:

FOR SARAH - WHEREVER SHE MAY BE

1. *I remember so many things. I can't see you, or touch you, so my memories will have to do.*

   I remember: the first words I said when you were born - 'Look, she's beautiful'
   > *being the first person to find out you had teeth - you bit me!*
   > *teaching you to dip french fries in your ketchup - and that gorgeous messyface afterward.*
   > *cleaning up after you at 3 a.m. when you wre so sick you needed a   bath.*
   > *singing 'I'm not small' for you in the car, on the way home from   daycare*

CHORUS:

   You've been taken away, my bright and shining star,
   But I'm thinking of you all the time, no matter where you are;
   So remember, darling daughter, if you ever think of me,
   I wrote these words for Sarah, wherever she may be.

2. *As the time passes, the memories I have become sharper, clearer, and infinitely more precious.*
   I remember:
   plucking caramels from you ear (simple sleight of hand)
   Sharing caramels and bubble gum.
   Telling you the story of Julie Ann and the mud puddle—

   just once, and having you remember it a week later
   Asking you for your promise, and hearing you say, oh so solemenly,

STREET PEOPLE SPEAK

'I promise!'
Cuddling you when you were scared by a television program - or when you just wanted to be held.

CHORUS:

3.   *Sometimes, sweetheart when life kicks me in the teeth, the only thing*
     that sustains me is the good times with you.
     I remember: How you asked to rest your head on my belly when we
     watched TV together.
     The day of the Children's Festival, when you were a clown, and we made
     a puppet together.
     Carrying you, almost asleep, from the car, you head on my shoulder.
     Kisses goodnight when little arms reached up around my neck and pulled
     our cheeks together in our own special 'minihug'
     Asking: 'What does a cheese monster say?'
     and hearing a two year old voice (trying to sound gruff) say:
     'Cheese, please!'
     Yes Sarah, they may take you away from me, but rest assured,
     In my heart of hearts I'll always be -
     your Daddy."

Ruth Morris and Colleen Heffren

Early morning breakfast for Toronto's homeless and time for social gathering. The Mission offers spiritual council and job referals in addition to breakfast.

CHAPTER TWO: WE BELIEVE

1. Best Things in Our Lives

Before we asked street people about the worst things about life on the street, we asked them what was best. Nearly a third, not surprisingly, said there was nothing "best" about it. The rest gave a wide range of answers. The freedom of street life topped the list (8%) with other responses following closely: just being still alive; hope; being with my children (for the family hostel); friends; family, and the ability to learn from it. For those who answered freedom it meant the freedom to come and go as they please, and to be themselves. Some of these street people had been in institutions and the street was a kind of reaction to the total control of institutional life. One person noted that the best things were:

"Music and PEOPLE. Amazing wonderful emotional feelings I don't want to trade!"

Looking on the bright side, a refugee said it was:

"Survivial: seeking a new life, liberty and peace."

Another person commented that he got more money and better treatment on the street than on welfare. Dave had warm memories of people who had been kind:

One day I asked someone for 60 cents and they gave me $5. I remember the good ones. One man took me out to a restaurant himself, and said, 'I'll buy you anything on the menu.' He bought me a steak dinner. I asked him for a cigarette, and he bought me three packages."

Several people expressed some contentment by reducing expectations:

"I don't expect great things from people, so therefore I'm not disappointed."

"The best thing is a quiet stairwell to sleep in, with nobody bothering me."

This epitome of modest expectations is touching, especially in contrast to the irony of Cory's reply:

"The oxygen is still breathable for now."

A few felt they had learned from their experiences and that this learning was, indeed, the best thing:

"I've been in this predicament so long, not just the housing but the whole thing, that I have grown wise. I don't let it get to me, and I never give up."

"I'm trying to enjoy life every day. I come into places like these and I resolve not to be like that. I live on HOPE."

2. Worst Things in our Lives

Lack of shelter topped the list of "worst" things - about one-third of the street people named it. Lack of money, unemployment, loneliness, and uncertainty followed in that order. Person after person pointed out the inextricable connection between the lack of housing, jobs and money. But it was the lack of housing that people identified as the one factor necessary to unravel it. This would seem to underline the point the "Homes First" coalition is making.

Some miss most the things they have to do without:

"Having to do without things I should have: a clean, warm place, a wife and family. I should have it and would have if it hadn't taken so long to recuperate from the shock treatments. I also miss a responsible job, and hate having to lie about the diagnosis and mental illness in order to try for jobs."

The loss is felt particularly by those who had it and then lost it:

"Having no TV, no radio, no car - like, I was moving ahead, had my biggest place so far, and then I lost it all. It's hard to move back."

Some worry about their lack of education, and a few alcholics are frightened by their blackouts, by not remembering what they have done in these periods.

A mundane but very serious annoyance for many is the struggle to keep oneself and one's clothes clean:

"There's no place to get clothes washed, because all you've got to wash is what you have on your back."

The sheer cost of finding a place to rent at any reasonable cost is a deep concern:

"It's worse now than ever. I've never seen it so bad. There's nothing around. I walked around with over $700 in my pocket and couldn't find anything. I could get a hotel room for $100 a week, but who can afford that? I see people sleeping in doorways, phone booths, parked cars in used lots - the situation is desparate."

Stan and Jerry both most mind the insecurity:

"It's the uncertainty. I don't know what is going to happen tomorrow. I could kill myself. I would never have dreamed five or six years ago that I would be here. I'm afraid of disease; I keep clean by paying twenty-five cents for baths whenever I can. I'm afraid of freezing to death."

"It's insecurity. I don't know what is going to happen. I am afraid of being beaten - there are dangerous gangs. People beat me because of the way I look. It's like there is a gang war, and I'm caught in the middle, without even caring about the issue."

Not unrelated are two comments which reflect the feeling that the worst thing is in people's attitudes toward them:

"The attitude, people's attitude. There's a lack of respect. There are a lot of people here who just can't find jobs. When the depression hit, the numbers went way up. Housing is incredibly inefficient or too expensive, and welfare housing rates are too low. It's the old no address, no money, no job dilemma."

"I get treated like a retard because I live at the Sally Ann. When I saw a cabbie being beaten by punkers, the cops made fun of me because I was at the Sally Ann. I get kicked out of shopping malls just for standing there."

This kind of rejection accentuates the loneliness which several people mentioned as their biggest grief:

STREET PEOPLE SPEAK

"Loneliness is the key. It's not only me in a city of three million. There is lots of loneliness, and fear of the unknown."

"It's not having somewhere to go, being lonely. That is what I really hate. It wasn't so bad when I had my own room, with my roomate coming home, and finding someone there. It scares me to find no one there. I am living on the street partly from fear of going to an empty room and being by myself. The TV and radio don't help this kind of isolation."

One of the street people concluded his statement on loneliness with a moving plea about loneliness everywhere and our need to break down barriers:

"There is a lot of loneliness among street people. They are outside; there is no opening for them. They need a normal life: give them room. Give them something to care for, to remind them they are human beings.

And we need to care not just for people on the streets, but for people in our neighbourhoods, people everywhere."

It is a long way from that kind of universal caring to the cold and weariness of the streets. The young man who spoke those words is on the streets tonight as I type this, enduring the conditions, described by Dave and Bob, two street veterans:

"It's the freezing cold, being chilled to my bones. It weakens my health, which is poor already..."

"Fatigue, continuous fatigue. It's a little better in good weather."

Two older men remind us what are the sorrows of those who find themselves on the streets in their old age:

"I have not so many friends because everybody die already. I don't tell nothing to nobody, cause I got nobody. Everybody die, my friends."

Stan, who spoke these words, is an old Polish immigrant, here for many years, with limited English. He was terribly dirty, bent, with reddish brown skin, a slouch hat and one of the most neglected looking people I interviewed. Finally, Parry describes it with the stoicism of an older native person:

"Nothing. I'm too old to care anymore."

3. Changing Ourselves

When we asked Jim if there was anything in himself he would like to change, he withdrew into his shell, muttering, "You don't like me." He was pathetic, mentally ill, barefoot, with a tattered jacket and filthy hands and feet. Most people were able to respond more positively to the question. About a quarter said there was nothing they wanted to change, but nearly 40% named some personal quality; 12% wanted to change their drinking; 6% wanted to get off the streets, and 6% wanted more education. Another pathetic lost and confused young person said:

"I can't save money. I need someone I can depend on to keep it, and not give it to me. I dream a lot - it's like thinking."

A considerable group of people were very concrete and courageous in saying they knew what needed changing - their drinking:

"I've no one to blame but myself because of drink. I started drinking from frustration, long hours hard work, and not getting anywhere financially."

"This drinking problem - the longer I'm out of the work force the harder my life is getting."

"When I first lived on the streets, I didn't care, because I had so much hate and anger from the divorce. Yet it was almost all my fault. WHY DO WE DESTROY IT WHEN WE HAVE WHAT WE REALLY WANT? I started drinking at thirteen, and never really stopped."

Others wanted to reject themselves and their lives totally. A woman with a fragmented past and present, a schizophrenic with no parents, who had lost her children, said:

"Everything. Be decent. Have just one man, take care of him, allow him to treat me good, and treat him good."

A man from an institutional background declared:

"I'd like to blow my head off - and I'd like to get off the street. That's all."

On a more positive note, a young man said:

"I'd like to go back to ten, and know the things I know now, so I wouldn't make the same mistakes!"

A number wanted to change their attitudes:

"I'm changing my attitude toward people now, caring more, putting others first."

"I want to change lots in myself. Once you are in prison, you get that 'f— you' attitude, and it tends to stay with you, and you resent the establishment."

An indication of some of the positive goals came from Mickey, a hostile, alienated young man whose earlier comments were mostly negative:

"I would like to get a trade to put my ideas to use to make money. I have a creative streak and need to apply it. I need to focus my talents industrially, take a designer's course and paint designs."

Clearly, many of the street people dream and some of their dreams include steadily working on themselves to make the changes happen to build the dreams.

4. Dealing with Depression

One of the most important questions we asked was: "when you are down, what keeps you going?" One of the greatest challenges is to learn to cope with being on the street, where one is surrounded by others engaged in conspicuous consumption who despise you for your lack of possessions and status. Our street people gave a wide range of answers to this question: support from friends or relatives, drinking, faith, avoiding thinking about it, acceptance, helping others, keeping busy, realizing others are even worse off than you. More specific answers included: crying, humour thinking of the future, music, anger or revenge, will to survive, or fear of death, patience, my baby, or my family.

One significant group of answers focussed on acceptance. Two people expressed acceptance along with their determination not to be on the street forever:

> "I never let myself get down. I also promised myself I would not act or talk street, so I don't."

> "I won't let myself get down - I just can't. I would get involved in games if I felt down. There is nothing that would bring myself out of it if I let myself get down. I keep alive and keep moving, and always remember that I don't want to stay here."

Sometimes, acceptance is based on the sheer will to survive:

> "It's my instinct for survival: the smell of my own body keeps me going."

"Just to survive. To survive is everything. I just get through the day the best I can. Read papers, go to the library. Above all, I don't dwell on troubles; I cope with them the best I can and try to survive."

Sometimes, living on the raw will to survive leads to ennuie::

"Do nothing. It just gets mechanical. I just keep going."

Tim described a whole range of emotions when you try to live just on acceptance:

"It's perpetual motion: you have no choice. Things can't get any worse. You are at the bottom already so there's nowhere to go but up. You do whatever you have to do.

You are so busy just staying alive on the street, worrying where you are going to sleep, and where you are going to eat that day.

But it is lonely sometimes. You have to be motivated when there is nothing to be motivated for. You spend most of the time fighting yourself. The prospects if you do get your head just above water aren't alluring either: the struggle to pay rent, to eat, just fighting to break even, when you can do that here for free. It is really hard to get ahead, either way, once you are down here!"

Charles, a young, unemployed black man, had his own version of the famous "Serenity Prayer:"

"If there is something I do know it is in my own attitude: I accept things. When you know you can do something, you work on a problem. But if it is beyond me, I walk away from it. Sometimes you have to stand up. You have to know when to stand up, and when to accept the situation."

Rob summarized the wisdom of two religions in this way:

"I think for me it is strong Christianity - that SUFFERING IS NORMAL. And the Ojibway religion teaches us this too. Nobody can knock me down, including myself."

Tar, a street musican, expressed a similar blend of stoicism and faith:

"Sheer persistence, patience, and faith."

Vince's answer could have passed for a Quaker's response:

"A little voice inside keeps me going: 'Stick with the light.'"

Alan described an experience when he had been really down. He had gone to church feeling suicidal. He put his last quarter in the collection box. The minister, after the service, called him by his real name, a name he no longer used. It seemed like a message of hope and it restored his will to live.

Some people noted their tendency to deal with depression by drinking but were aware that the troubles were there in redoubled strength when they came out of the alcoholic stupor.

Donald felt it was a sense of balance that sustained him:

"The thought that there is always another side to life keeps me going."

Jim, on the other hand, used humour to ward off the temptation to drink:

"I try not to get down - I joke a lot. You get to a certain point and you will drink to forget. You sense what it could do to you if you take it too seriously. The whole system dehumanizes you.

You have to treat it like first down in a game. But IT treats YOU like last down."

When you have the weight of street life facing you each day, with pressure and failure, it is difficult to carry on. Some, like Stan, fantasize to escape mentally:

"I still fantasize: there is hope. It doesn't look too good, but when I daydream I FEEL good - thinking about what I don't have: a nice home, clothes, a good wife, and friends."

Others are driven still further into the realm of fantasy. Those who had retreatd into the realm of mental illness had their own response:

I keep my hopes on tomorrow, wishing my problems away from me. Optimism kills the delusions of the dark burdens weighing on me."

"Staying in hostels, thieves come around me, stealing the bit I have, and making scenes they can through me, with them."

This last quotation reminds us chllingly of the plight of mentally ill persons who are least able to cope even with a protective environment. Often they are shunted into the street where they are surrounded by every kind of danger and difficulty. Their shadowy world is crushed by the harsh reality all around them. Perhaps, the most positive response by one of those struggling with mental illness on the street was from Ron:

"I survived by stopping trying to please my parents!"

Others kept going because of the support of friends:

"Friends help me survive; people who can understand

> and care to ask when they see me down. One friend is constantly concerned about my well being. He has a home, and helps me."

Such friends are, alas, too rare.

Some people remembered that there were people even worse off then they:

> "I have seen people in lots worse condition than me in the hostels. The key is getting my fifteenth or sixteenth wind. There is a reason for being here. I'm going to stick around long enough to find it."

> "I just think of people worse off than myself. One time I went in a store, and the owner had no legs. Then I met his partner, who had one arm. Everybody there had some handicap. I found out they were veterans crippled by war, and instead of feeling sorry for themselves, they organized this business to employ other handicapped. I felt down before I walked in there, but I felt great after. It's the old story, 'I cried because I had no shoes till I met a man who had no feet.'"

One man, with many years on the street, lives only to help others, and with the support of his faith:

> "I know people who need help. This and my faith keep me going. When I am really down I read the Bible, and keep going. But I don't belong to any church. The church makes rules, and I don't want to be under rules in order to be a Christian. Religion is open to everybody.
>
> Some people on the streets who say they are not Christians are more Christian than Christians."

Young Jerry gave me the thought which we promised him would end this section. When asked how he survived the down times, he gave me his smile, which was peculiarly sweet. He said:

STREET PEOPLE SPEAK

"I occasionally get on a depression-suicide trip. Then I think:

'There is a place I am going to miss if I leave now.

There is a person I should know, that I am not going to see.'

There is too much I want to do for me to give up. It's a copout to kill yourself. If I can grow and explore, then I have lived. I have never yet done the things I want to do."

He was living proof of his own philosophy. If he had given up earlier, he would not have been there that day to share those beautiful words with the people who may read them in this book. We were all meant to know Jerry, and to absorb, through him, the faith of a child on the street.

5. Our Dreams: Three Magic Wishes

We asked our street people "if you were offered three magic wishes, anything at all you wanted, what would you choose?" Some of them had difficulty responding. One laughed and asked if this was a joke. Another observed that wishes never came true. A third said he wouldn't want a magic wand, as he wanted to live the way God wished him to. He was a schizophrenic who had tried drugs and alcohol, but now was struggling to accept whatever harsh reality life offered him. One of the more inventive dreamers asked first for three magic wands! He than wished for equality and happiness for everyone in the world. His one concrete, personal wish was for a decent job.

A number of the homeless combined wishes for the good of others, or the world at large, with personal needs. Two-thirds of them had at least one wish for the world, at large, or others outside themselves. The largest group of wishes, 43%, were for stable housing. About one-third wished for an adequate income; 30% for a job; and 17% for good health.

Ruth Morris and Colleen Heffren

There was an understandable tendency to wish for decent housing or some other personal need first. But the extent of altruism among people in such dire need is astonishing. The overwhelming yearning for a good place to live, seldom expressed in fancy or luxurious terms, denies the myth that street people choose the street. The yearning for a decent, steady job is also significant. Many people expressed their wish simply for a good family life.

Wishes for the world at large included world peace, no nuclear weapons, no pollution, housing for the homeless everywhere, world prosperity, an end to poverty everywhere, and the equalization of power. Several wanted to help keep people off the street, either by providing housing, or by helping with social and emotional stresses. After asking for the equalization of power throughout society, mental stability for everyone and a world all blue, (he was an artist, and spoke of the psychological meaning of blue), Rob added:

> "I would change the world: no more piecemeal economics, no more of this eventual stuff. Everyone would have respect. We have enough technology to solve every problem in the world. We need to have contact with the disparities in the world."

Will asked to sit in the Prime Minister's seat for six months to put the country back where it should be, especially in building appropriate housing for the needy. He then wanted the healing power to repair the emotional damage already done. Finally, he showed recognition of the burdens of government, by asking for this third wish:

> "To give the job back to someone else, so I can start living too!"

Bob's first wish was to use his power to MAKE us understand:

STREET PEOPLE SPEAK

"I'd wish for an earthquake and a hurricane in Toronto for three days, so the WHOLE POPULATION WOULD KNOW WHAT IT IS LIKE IN WINTERTIME AT TWENTY BELOW."

However, with his second wish, he turned this into a dream we would all have simultaneously, so that the real suffering would not have to take place. Bob was not prepared to let the rest of the word suffer what the world has already let him suffer, despite his deep desire for us to understand and care.

Another entire group of people asked for relationships: past, present and future:

"My mother back alive."

"Somebody who loves me and that I love and could trust; just to be decently happy - I'm not happy; I'm lonely."

"A social life, family, and children, and to stay sober."

"To find my sister NOW."

"For my four year old son to be a smart kid, and that he have a chance in life, and me too."

"A place to stay, happier days, and a baby." (homeless couple).

"To be back with my wife, but I wouldn't tell her that!"

Many wishes were for the basic needs of life. What was most striking was how modest many of them were. It was almost as if they had been conditioned by their harsh reality not to ask for much. Dick's three wishes are highlighted by their "reasonableness":

"A day job at reasonable pay.

> A reasonable place to live.
> A little happiness. They weren't all like that in my 20's!'"

Other wishes were also moving in their simplicity::

> "Enough money to live decently, so I would not have to go to missions. A nice suit, shoes, and to be able to shower every day."

> "Not to be a millionaire, but not being on the streets. I've looked at people and cried: people who have given up hope. I don't want to get that far down, where you lose all hope.'"

> "To buy a little place where I can have my animals, and live there."

> "To have a permanent address, a healthy place to live, without bugs."

> "A home, and no epilepsy."

A number of the alcoholics expressed a desire to be able to stop drinking. Some of the native people wished to return to more traditional life. One wanted to go fishing and hunting. Another said:

> "I wish I owned Center Island, so I could use my boat. It isn't as far as Manitoulin Island. Or I'd like to go home, and put my boat in the water. And I'd like to quit drinking."

One father of a homeless family felt so exorcized over wanting to help people understand the tragedy homeless people experience that he wished to write a book about it. But the most devastating response came from one young man who summarized his three wishes this way:

> "Not to be born. It would be a lot easier. That's all."

STREET PEOPLE SPEAK

What do you say to a young man who tells you the world has turned his dreams of youth into only this desire? It was one of those remarks which stops an interview and leaves the interviewer wordless. Someone has entrusted you with their most bitter pain!

The "feminization" of poverty forces many woman into the streets seeking small comfort in Toronto's Cabbagetown park benches.

Ruth Morris and Colleen Heffren

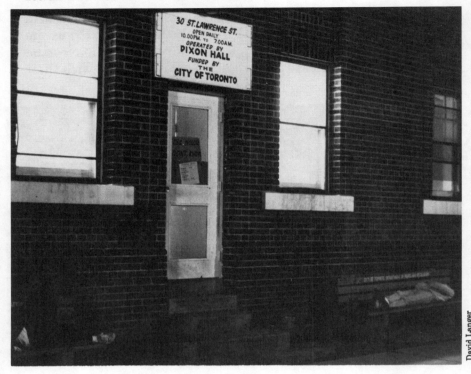

Toronto's Dixon Hall shelter is full and there are only outdoor spaces.

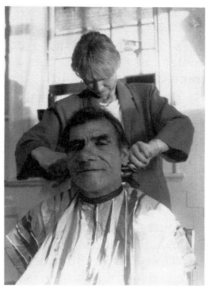

CHAPTER THREE:
WHERE WE COME FROM: BACKGROUND

1. How We Got Here

"I was raised as a foster child from ten to twelve. When I was twelve, I moved in with my Mom again, but my stepfather molested me. At fourteen, I went back to my foster family, but my foster father moelested me too, so I went to another home. At sixteen, I went back to Mom. Then I came to Toronto where I met Bob. We stayed with friends of his who were drug addicts. We moved to Parry Sound, and Mom threw Bob out cause he didn't have a job, and threw me out becaue I was engaged to him. We married at seventeen and twenty-four. We had two kids right away, living in a cold trailer. It was

57

bitterly cold. The kids have had a whole series of accidents and illnesses..."

This woman's shocking childhood demonstrates that many of the homeless never had a start in life before they landed in the street. Others had a little, and lost it, while a third group had quite a lot and, by some unlucky break, or by their own failure, lost it.

NEVER HAD IT

It takes a lot to get women into a life on the streets. Typical was Dorothy:

"When I was fourteen, my mother's boyfriend found out I was epileptic, and he abused me sexually off and on for eleven years. The police wouldn't believe me, and finally, told me not to call again. Then I was abused again in a Children's Aid home. I got thrown out of school for missing too many classes from the epilepsy and abuse problems. I was in a car accident when seven, had petit-mal from then on, grand mal from sixteen."

Native people on the street are another group whose lives are often poignant examples of never having had anything. We first met Weaver on the street, organizing street natives to do volunteer work for a service project. By the time we wanted to interview him, he was in jail. His affability and depth had come through his chronic alcoholic fog on the street. But his whole life had been saturated by alcohol, trying to drown the memories of all that the native people have lost.

"More than anything, I wish I had gone further in school. My whole life would have been different if I had. I dropped out in Grade 10, was drinking already, but didn't realize it was a problem. I never saw a native teacher till Grade 4, and the teachers didn't understand us much.

Dad and Mom were bootleggers. My father drank a lot but I didn't really know him after I was eight. One night somebody reported he was with a woman who had died, and he was scared of being charged so he disappeared. I never saw him again till I was eighteen. I didn't recognize him, but somebody pointed him out to me.

I talked to him and we had a coffee. 'Are you my son?'

'Well, I gues so. The guy said you are Bill Deerhunter.' It's a long story. Doesn't really bother me.

I came to Toronto when I was nineteen, started working, but I lost my first job from drinking, got paid every night, drank every night. By the time I realized drinking was a problem and tried to stop, I couldn't. Some of my friends have already died on the streets from it, drunk or frozen. I don't blame nobody for my life, it's me, drinking."

GC is a younger native still in his early twenties. His family history is littered with alcoholism and jails:

When I was fourteen, my father died from a fight on the street when he was drunk. Then I was seventeen, my mother died a violent death when she was drinking. My brothers and sisters all drink a lot too. From the time my father died, I began spending some time on the streets. When my mother died, I spent most of it. I'm not close to my brothers and sisters. I got welfare for a while, but it doesn't cover the cost of my room. I've done some volunteer work with native people and want to help my people, but I feel so much anger when people treat me like dirt."

Like most of the those who never had a start, GC has almost no job skills and few realistic good chances in life. These kinds of bad starts in life are not limited to women and native people. Many WASPS and immigrant males have them too.

From the age of twelve, Doug had to be the man of the house, looking after his sisters and brothers. He observed:

> "I was never a kid when I needed to be a kid, and I got into trouble. By the time I was 14 I was in reform school. Then just when I got out and needed help from my family, Mom moved out west and left me in an apartment all by myself. I'm the oldest of ten kids."

Vince also ran into problems very early in life:

> "I got into alcohol and drugs very early. My childhood memories are a mixture of boarding homes, group homes, being locked up for my schizophrenia, terrible confusion, and running away. But I did eventually get some survival techniques, partly from group therapy. I'm still on the street, but I'm more satisfied with myself now."

Vince shows more strength than some. Many who never had anything have spent their lives in the shadowland between institutions and the street. Penetang (the Ontario institution for the criminally insane), is a common stop for a number of them. They are delicately balanced between prisons, mental hospitals and street, but really fitting nowhere and desperately unhappy everywhere. Suicide attempts are common and their lives often end early as bleak proof of the sincerity of these attempts. Mark describes his life's boundaries:

> "My father used to beat my brother and me. When I was 16, my brother and I left home and started crashing in vagrant houses, taking drugs which helped me feel less depressed. I spent seven years on speed, sold it to support my habit, became so thin I was like a skeleton. I had so many shock treatments in mental hospital I was too cracked up for Guelph prison; they sent me to Penetang instead. Just the thought of being cooped up again sends me right to the bottle. I spent ten years in Penetang, and I'm never going back there."

Mark has packed a lot in his 35 years of life, things that most of us have missed. But he has also missed a lot most of us have known, the very things that enable us to escape his perpetual street-institution existence.

STREET PEOPLE SPEAK

Ben R and Teddy are two men who never lost much because they started with nothing to lose. Ben's early life resembled that of some of the women. Childhood rape was a major influence on him and throughout his interview he was obsessed with the topic of the rape of young boys:

> "I got raped first when I was eleven. I used to run away from home because I couldn't stand the beatings from my stepfather. One night he came after me with a butcher knife; then I went for him with a cleaver. Sure, he was a drinker, but it went deeper than that. Mom got pregnant by this guy when I was two. He hated my real father, and I was never good enough to be with his darling little kids. I never saw my real father much till I was seventeen - he was an alcoholic too.
>
> When I was sixteen I got sent to Guelph prison. I got raped five times there. Then they sent me to Millbrook, maximum security and almost round the clock lockup, and they put me in the sex area cause I had already got screwed. I hate talking about myself...I'm trying desperately to stay out of prison as long as I can this time."

There is a humble realism to that "as long as I can" goal for Ben. Teddy has the earliest memories of major traumas of anyone we talked with:

> "I was brought up in Toronto. When I was four, I tried to choke a kid in Jr. kindergarten in the line, and I went into a children's institution. I did break and enters then too. I stayed there till I was eight. By then I was into arson and petty theft. I went for someone with a hockey stick cause he called my brother fatso. Like my Dad, I have a pretty nasty temper. Not too long till I was back in an institution where I learned how to do break and enters, rob grocery stores, and pick locks. I also learned how to make and use different kinds of drugs, and how to escape."

This remarkably versatile, liberal education was not in any way redirected by Teddy's experiences in school:

> "I was a slow learner and was always being flunked, and my parents expected me to do better. Then with going into institutions, I got more labelled and more confused and angry."

It is hard to know who is responsible for lives like Ben's and Teddy's. Children who are the objects of violence in childhood are likely to pass on the violence in adulthood and the chain of violence is hard to break. The one certainty is that the past, present, and future for Ben and Teddy are equally bleak. Neither prisons nor the street offer either of them or society any change from these steadily negative patterns.

HAD A LITTLE, LOST EVEN THAT

The line between this group and the other two is thin at times. Walt R, for example, never had much. But he described a little family life before disaster struck:

> "I was put in mental hospital, given electroshock till I was almost a vegetable. I asked for help and this is what I got. I refused treatment later, and they forced me. Now, at twenty-six, I am labelled permanently unemployable. I'm trying to get on disability. I can afford a room on disability."

Jerry was the youngest person we interviewed. At sixteen, he has already been on the streets for two years. He certainly had some start, but he lost it early and totally:

> "I'm the only son of upper middle class, professional parents. But I never could relate to them well. I dressed punk, and they couldn't stand that. They assumed I was even more rebellious than I was. I resented authority, especially school, I felt there should be a reason behind why we do things, not just 'because I say so.' When I was fourteen, I was on the run and got picked up. My Dad put

me in the car, took me to Children's Aid, and said, 'Take him, I don't want him.'"

The street was the bottom into which this rebellious, rejected child fell. And he is there still.

Several of the native people also had had a little and lost it. Typical was Ab, who only hit the street after the death of his mother and a move to Toronto which left him unemployed and without supports. Chuck, on the other hand, fell into the street after a divorce from his wife:

> "Alcohol was a problem before, but it got a lot worse after the divorce. Family was everything to me. I felt floating and abandoned in life, all my real ties cut off. I got some psychiataric help, spent some time in the Queen Street Mental Hospital, got into violent fights on the street. I'm still wavering emotionally."

Lloyd was a native who had relatively little, ever. As a child, he suffered abuse in an environment of alcoholism, unemployment and parents after times in jail. But he was able to make a start with marriage and a life with his five children, whom he loves deeply and speaks of emotionally.

Divorce changed all that. Lloyd could barely control his tears as he spoke of his losses, but tried to express himself positively:

> "Living poor so many years, the street don't seem quite so bad. The world of the street is home to me, instead of the home I had and loved and lost."

Lou provided a touch of humour in this depressing sequence. He came to Toronto in 1985 on a holiday, spent too much and has been on the street ever since! Todd on the other hand, kept moving, but had had no better success in finding work. He reported:

Ruth Morris and Colleen Heffren

"I've been on the streets and hostels the past six years. Only kind of jobs I ever get is $3.50 an hour. Went to Vancouver to look for work, but there was no work there. Then got back here with no money for a room. Finally, I got a job, but then it turned out to be temporary. So I'm back on the street."

Pat was one of a number who, far from depending on welfare, refused to apply for it:

"I lost a job four years ago, when I was eighteen, and didn't pick myself up right away. I never applied for UIC though I was entitled to it. I can't be bothered with the government, welfare or anything else. I work when I can and am trying to get more training to get back to regular work."

Donald was a man we knew for a few months. In his twenties, his shaggy looks and red, weatherbeaten face give him an indeterminate age in appearance. Like many of our street friends, he appeared and disappeared in our lives, and we wondered sometimes when we saw his feet dragging even more, his eyes even heavier, his shyness even more pronounced, where he had been in the long nights between our meetings. Donald has a story similar to many:

"I came from the west, have relatives out there. My sister and I were very close, though my parents are dead, and they never had much. I finished high school and took a course in food management. I got a job at a restaurant and even got a promotion. Then they wanted me to work extra hours for no more pay, and started making other demands that weren't fair. I quit. I'd been working eight years then, and I never dreamed I wouldn't get another job. I was on UIC a whole year, then it ran out. Then I got social assistance most of 1985, but I got cut off in October. I was still trying for jobs but I needed higher training for most jobs by then. And I was beginning to look a little seedy. Then without assistance, I lost my room in January 1986, and I've been on the streets ever since.

I did make one last effort before I was evicted, I got a welfare worker to try to find out why I had been cut off. She promised action, and just disappeared."

WE SLID AND LOST IT

Ralph was one of several who felt most of his troubles came from being unable to assert himself:

"My Dad died, and left everything he had to me. But it wasn't enough to cover the cost of his funeral. Then everybody took me for a ride moneywise. I can't say no to anybody. I gave away most of what I had to my sisters and brother, and they still abused me. Then when my marriage broke up and I had no home, nobody helped me."

Sol was an immigrant who had had everything - a good job, a wife, a two-bedroom apartment, colour TV, grown son, and, in common with many good Canadians, a minor drinking problem. Then as he neared fifty, things began piling up on him:

"First, my wife died. I kept working, but my drinking got worse. I moved to a smaller place, and drank more. Then three years ago I quit the good job I had, and began working just occasionally. I had a fight with the man who owned the small business where I worked. And now I've ended up here."

Many had experienced traumas but took full responsibility for their plight themselves. When he was young, Sol had been imprisoned as a political prisoner, had been a refugee, later was deeply shocked by the loss of his wife and had been abandoned by his grown son. But he blamed only himself and his failure to control his drinking for his plight.

Mickey was another eager, would-be-worker who lost out in the trek between Vancouver and Toronto, looking for work in both places:

> "When there wasn't any work out there, I packed up two bags of clothes and came back here. I asked a friend to get them while I was working at a temporary job, but he forgot and I lost them. In the past, I worked full-time for eight years in a mill for $11.00 an hour. But now I've got to head back to Vancouver to try to survive. It's a bind I need $200.00 to go back by bus, four days."

Carol was one of the most unlikely looking people we talked with. With a quiet elegance of class, more like a movie star or fashion model, than someone on the edge of hostel life, she was a grim reminder that it can happen to anyone. From a solid immigrant background, she married a man with a big front, of whom her family disapproved:

> "My husband had a big income, but he was a big spender too. After a few years, his business went bankrupt, and he left me and our little boy for his secretary. He went off to Europe with her, and left me here to cope. He and his family managed to get all the equity from our house and left me with nothing. My family were still blaming me for marrying him, and they said, 'You made your bed, you lie on it.'"

Carol's husband had always objected to her working while they were married. Now she was making plans to get back to work. She and her little boy were living on welfare and had to adjust to their totally changed lives.

Jack had a jaunty air and a lot of jokes. These enabled him to deal with his frustrations at the losses and incongruities he had experienced in recent years. As he said:

> "I had it all: a three bedroom house, wife, daughter, dog, camper trailer, and expense account at work, and I lost everything. My wife divorced me, we had a terrible divorce. In the flurry of legal bills, I made a terrible mistake. I accepted UIC while I was still working. They caught me, and I was given a $250 fine or ninety days. I

had no choice, I served the ninety days, and when I got out, just like the ad says, the punishment began. I had lost my room, and now I'm in this impossible no room-no job bind."

Andre lost it more abruptly:

"I was working at a good job at $15 an hour. I was there for nine years. They promoted a guy who had been there much less over my head, and he was kind of arrogant. One time he put his hand on me. I changed shifts every week, the work was very demanding and dangerous, lot of guys lost fingers, and I was too edgy. I lost my temper and hit him. The next day I was fired for it. That guy did the same thing, putting his hand on a woman later, and she kept her cool and reported him and he got fired. But it didn't do me any good.
Then my fiancee got pregnant, we wanted the baby, so we had to get married, even with me unemployed. It's so hard to lose a really good job. Even a month before it happened, I wouldn't have believed it could happen to anybody. Now here we are without a home for our baby. It's hard to try to get back at my age when you have lost everything. If I had been twenty-six, it would have been easier. Also, it is a terrible strain for my wife and on our new marriage."

The slide into the street is not easy, whether you have never known a home or family supports most of us take for granted, or whether you have tasted a little security and happiness, or whether you have had a large taste of "success", and then the bottom suddenly falls out. Whichever way it happens, it is important to look at the kind of childhoods and families street people have experienced.

2. Our Feelings Toward Family

Many of the family histories are depressing sagas of those who never had warmth or stability yet they have powerful emotions about their families. Alan is a native person whose life was obviously coloured by his family:

> "There was a lot of violence in our family, my parents fighting each other, and beating us. Most of us drink a lot and use drugs. My father went to jail in 1945, and the family had to scatter and sleep outside. We put our things in an old car and slept in it in February. Then later, my mother went to jail too. But I'm close to my family, I love them, and I like to see them."

One of the most poignant comments on the fostering system came from another native person, Spic, who said:

> "I've been in too many foster homes. I don't remember who my foster parents were. Drink is all that makes my life livable."

Most street people had strong memories of their own families. Many of them were bitter:

> "I couldn't care a damn whether they all die and go to Hell. Everything has always been bad for me."

> "They don't know if I'm dead or alive. I'd be better off in prison."

> "My family doesn't care. All they ever try is the sarcastic treatment."

> "I've been epileptic since six months of age, was in a boys' home for nine years. My parents are the cause of my being on the streets. I would talk to my sister if I was really desperate."

> "Sometimes I do contact my parents. They are scum, not caring, have a phony image. I'm a little closer to my father than my mother. I was shafted and thrown out. They should be charged for emotional crimes. They know nothing about life, really."

"My parents hated us. My father beat all of us brutally. My brother is living under the Dundas viaduct, in the ravine. He almost lost his hand in a machine accident. He cracked up, and lives a desolate, vile existence. My parents had me locked up in a nuthouse. They care nothing for any of us."

One woman stated:

"My parents never liked me. It was my brother my parents adored. I give my kids what I never had. I never spent one Christmas with my parents. I was always sent to my cousins'."

Some had more trouble with one parent than with the other. Bill observed:

"My father was very screwed up, but he handles it very well. He screws up others worse than himself. I was in a psychiatric ward when I was 14, and daycamp for emtionally disturbed kids."

Mark also saw his father at the centre of the family's problems:

"My father had a drinking problem. I was the oldest of seven, but am not in touch with any of my family now. My father threw me out when I was 15, and I've been on the streets ever since. Mom used to sneak me in to sleep in the basement sometimes. I was in an opportunity class for slow learners because of the home problems. Mom died of cancer two years ago."

Others saw their mother as the root of their problem. One young woman, a diagnosed psychopath, described her family life this way:

"My mother had lots of sex and lots of kids. My sister was adopted and I never even saw her. My mother died when

I was thirteen. I was put in an orphanage and they threw me out at fourteen. I have no idea where my father is. My own three kids were put up for adoption."

An immigrant man expressed his anger at his mother:

"Mother was very arrogant and dominating. She tried to run my life. I feel so angry I want to kill her. She is always driving me to do something more. She nags and argues constantly and is very possesive. She has destroyed my brother's mind, calling him bad for petty things."

George described a common pattern, where a physical handicap seems to provoke familial and other abuse, leading to further problems that provoke still worse abuse:

"As a child, I was abused because I was partially crippled. I am now more disabled from that abuse by my parents. I tried to kill myself at ten. I've been drugged, raped, molested, and abused many times by men at parties. I want a sex change so men will leave me alone.

I was a slow learner. I was abused in the group home I was in and wouldn't go to another one, as I was too afraid. Now I can't find a job because I use a cane, and because with the things I've been through, it is hard to seem employable."

Not all street people have had devastatingly deprived family lives. Stan spent four years in Eastern European prisons for trying to cross the border, beginning when he was just nineteen.

A number of people identified strengths of one parent, who provided much appreciated love and stability. Theo spoke movingly of his mother:

"My father was an alcoholic who died at forty-five. He had cancer and emphysema, and drank very heavily. My mother worked from 9 a.m. till 11 p.m. to support us. She raised four of us by herself."

Others like young Jerry, though feeling rejected or neglected by their families, appreciated that it is sometimes a two way street.

"My parents hurt me a lot, but I hurt them back. I have some grudges against people. Maybe someday we can talk again."

When it comes to contact with their families of origin, our street people have three kinds of positions: warmth, coolness, or an unwillingness to intrude. Despite painful childhoods, a number of native people cherish warm feelings toward their family. Two of them observed:

"I have regular contact with all but one of my brothers and sisters. They are very nice. I don't go to their places when I am tipping the bottle, but otherwise we are close. Only one brother is on the street like me, the rest have homes."

"I sometimes phone my brother in Manitoulin Island. I feel very close to my relatives. They are special."

Parry, a young black man, also described family relations as very close and very important. He kept in touch with all his brothers and sisters and felt good about the way each of them related to him.

Cooler responses came from people like Reed, with his "distance makes the heart grow fonder" philosophy:

"As long as I don't have to live with them, I get along just great with them!"

Dennis described his feelings with less humour and more aloofness:

"I have some contact, but I feel toward them as much love

as for all life. But my love has to stay inside because there is too much hatred and greed outside. My warm feelings have to remain hidden or I'd get hurt."

Dick brought the same sense of coldness and distance to his feelings toward family:

"They are like some kind of people I read about in books: fictional, distant and cold."

A third quite numerous group of people, kept some distance from their family, perhaps out of a sense of pride and shame. They did not want their family to see them so down and out. They preferred to wait to have contact until they could show up triumphant, a success after all. At the very least, they did not want to be a burden. Martin, who has supported himself all his life, did not want to be dependent:

"I feel O.K. about my family, no problems. I'm easygoing, but I don't want to be a burden to them. I want to make my own way. I've painted houses 40 years, but have a bad spine now, and my legs are giving out. I've been on medical welfare for two years now."

Martin's situation raises the interesting question: why ARE people like this, who have worked hard all their lives, falling into the cracks and into the street in their old age? Why do we as a society, make them ashamed of the natural dependence of old age and illness after a lifetime of toil?

Another man, only 35, who took to drink after a divorce, was too ashamed to call relatives, although he felt good toward them. One of the most aimiable alcoholics we met observed:

"I would contact them when I am together. No use asking help now - I would be a hopeless cause!"

Neil, a husband who was experiencing the heartache of seeing not only himself but his family homeless, had thought deeply about this issue:

STREET PEOPLE SPEAK

"My friends and family have not been very supportive. My family are very well off. It's easy for anyone to say 'come and stay with us. But instead, they left us here, which creates more problems. We see my family, yet I feel very bitter about them right now. I'm still pleasant if they call, but I feel a lot of resentment because I WOULD NOT HAVE SEEN THIS HAPPEN TO THEM. They wouldn't even keep my furniture, so I lost it.

One uncle has been very nice. He and I have always been specially close, and I helped him through a crisis once.

But I've been doing some soul searching about how it could be. I think it's part of the decay of the family. My father is seventy-one, but I'll never see him in this position. How many Chinese have you interviewed for this book? They still believe in their roots."

But family backgrounds and family feelings are only one part of the picture.

3. Why We're On the Street

Street people felt they were on the street for a wide variety of reasons. Some of them again identified tough starts in life:

"Children's Aid. Where do you go from Children's Aid? I felt they weren't helping me."

"My parents died when I was fifteen. My older brothers and sisters were married. I was the black sheep."
This black sheep was terribly dirty, with a long beard and hair, tattered shoes and jacket. It reminded one of his long years on the street.

A number of people blamed directly their own drinking with words such as these:

"Alcohol, having a hard time managing money. I'd sooner go drink than do the right things."

"Had to do it my way: drugs and booze. I got sick."

"I don't blame it on nobody: it's ME. Drinking. When I was in Oshawa doing volunteer work with native groups, and sober myself, I saw drunks, and I could see how I am when I'm drunk."

Others blamed themselves for other things:

"The things I blame for my being here are: first me; second, my father; the economic environment; my low job skills; my affinity for alienating people - but not intentionally; but I'm hoping to turn it around, as I'm involved in helping set up the new cooperative apartment complex, geared to income. I'm working on the committee."

This young man was a gifted child who, like a number of gifted children, had trouble in a school environment that was no more adapted to gifted children than to other special needs. He also had a difficult home environment. His efforts to help both himself and others through supporting new housing initiatives were heartening.

Another man blamed himself with these words:

"I put myself here. Also other people and my family put me here: attitdues, don't care attitudes by both them and me."

Some were handicapped by literacy problems:

"Literacy. Can't spell though I can read some, but I can't get a job because of my spelling."

A great number understood the cycle of no job - no home - no money. A young native person observed:

STREET PEOPLE SPEAK

"Lack of job skills, no job experience, not enough education. Emotional setbacks and frustrations. I'd like my life to be different, to be able to have respectability and a place in the community."

"Can't get a place without a job. Everything is connected, and I can't move out of it."

"Lack of a base. Lack of first and last. Without welfare I would probably have been in jail."

Some focussed more specifically on the employers' job market, which gives employers all the choices and leaves these low status, powerless people in a situation with only poor paying, unstable, unpleasant job choices. Paul, a very bright and disillusioned young member of our army of young unemployed people, commented:

"It's employers refusing work, and their attitudes toward employees. 'Who care about you. I've got 20 people waiting to fill your position.'"

Tom felt a similar discouragement which damped his enthusiasm for the struggle necessary to get work:

"There's nothing to work for. It's not much use working at a job where the money won't last: low pay, no security."

This lack of incentives creates a lack of real choices. These street youth often felt they could only choose from degrees of marginalitiy. But older workers who had lost jobs agonizingly blamed themselves again and again for not realizing how hard it would be to get another:

"It's the job situation, and my not having enough foresight to see this could have happened, that I could be unable to get another job for this long."

Len summed up his situation wittily:

"There's two causes: annual income deficiency, and my parents."

Bill, who had spent years between institutions and the street, had a thoughtful analysis and still had his dreams as well:

"It's partly lack of money. Also, other people not really being there to help in my childhood, but blaming the past isn't going to get anywhere. If I could find someone to really care, I'd be O.K. If I could get $50,000, I'd open a house for people like myself, with a living room and openness..."

Another blamed the housing shortage more directly:

"I've been on the waiting list for four years for a public housing apartment. It's the shortage of places, and being hard up."

Dick is one of the many who got caught in their own efforts to follow the shifting geography of jobs:

"I haven't worked fulltime since February, 1986. My Dad thought there were better jobs in Toronto, and urged me to move here. I expected to get a job in a month. I stayed with my sister temporarily. I'm still on UIC, but it takes a month to transfer it. I had no idea jobs and housing were so awful here. I resent having to worry more about a place to live than finding a suitable job. I make two job applications, and then have to stop in the middle to look for places to live. I'm not eating very well. The strain is terrible."

One of the burning issues in this area is whether some people "choose" the street. Tar is a good example of someone who appears to have done so:

"I'm a street musician. In order to play music my way, without my creativity being stifled, I choose to play on the street. I refuse to be compromised, so I prefer the street."

But as one of the people who runs a drop-in commented:

"I resent our calling it a choice. Sure some of them 'choose' the street, but they choose from a set of lousy choices. How do you choose between a totally abusive home and the street or between hopeless unemployment and rejection, and the street? Choosing the street is a bad joke."

Marty agreed with this, observing:

"It's not because I like it. There are times when I just HATE it."

Fred is one of the older people on the street, many of whom are not drinkers, who have become castoff before sixty-five either by ill health, disability, automation in the workplace or just plain changing times. Low as our pensions are, these men look forward to turning sixty-five as a respite from their present straits. Fred comments on his situation:

"I only got a Grade 8 education because I left school to help my family, and in those days that wasn't so bad anyway. I drove trucks all my life, but now I'm sixty-one, and I got flebitis in both my legs. My circulation is bad, and I can't walk much. I go in and out of hospital, and last month someone stole my check. Now I'm on the street."

Mickey was bitter. He blamed society for rejecting him because he was different:

> "People crush out what they are afraid of, and people are afraid of me. I dress different, I look different, I am different, so they are afraid, and they want to crush me, like I was a bug."

Charles, a young black, asked the age-old questions about the existence of evil in a world he still wanted to believe is created by a good and caring God:

> "I believe there is a God. But why does God do things this way? Time just keeps going on, and things don't get better. There a few things I just don't understand, like -

> 'Why is there discrimination?' and

> 'Why are we on the street?'"

How does one respond to a question like this from a young man who has had few opportunities and has even fewer future prospects?

One native person, Rob, came up with a whimsically accurate answer:

> "It's people teaching us how to get off the reservations! The government wants us off, and told us it's easy. It's cheaper to administer us through mainstream society. They are welcoming us with open arms in their own unique way."

Finally, Will and Derek expressed considerable alienation from society in their conclusions. Will blamed our social values:

> "I did't understand society. I didn't understand that money was more valuable than life. There is nothing to pick you up but you."

Derek began with a sardonic comment on his early judgment on school:

"I never trusted my own judgment at five or six. I didn't like school, but believed they knew best. I'm not a conventional person, and I should have believed my own judgment.

It was not knowing who I really was. I had inflated expectations from my parents, and was confused. Later alcoholism and the rheumatoid arthritis that the doctors accused me of malingering with made me bitter. I had to get away from people, because I don't want to explain I am in pain. I am suffering from emotional and mental exhaustion. Unemployment is just one effect of all this."

Derek obviously had a good deal of insight, along with a frankly astringent philosophy.

The street people we talked with came from all over the world, but about three-quarters were of Canadian origin. About 30% of the whole group were native Torontonians and about 10% each were born in Manitoulin Island (natives), other parts of Ontario, the Canadian East and other parts of Canada. The great majority, about 70% were in their twenties and thirties, contrary to the image of the old drunk in the gutter. About 55% were Canadian whites, and another 15% European whites. Twenty percent were native people and the remaining 10%, black or Latin American.

Contrary again to the popular image of alcohol as the major and almost sole cause of being on the street, unemployment and lack of housing ranked as primary causes. Although alcohol was important in many life tragedies, bitterly traumatic childhoods and broken marriages in adult life had major impacts on many lives. The lack of suitable housing for ex-mental patients and for ex-convicts was also important.

This is where our street people came from. Now we can look at how they confront the world.

Ruth Morris and Colleen Heffren

The hard, isolated park bench a momentary stop for the homeless is something that school dosen't prepare you for.

CHAPTER FOUR:
MEETING THE WORLD

1. School

A part of our sterotyped image of street people is that they are uneducated drunks, dregs of society whom we can hardly imagine as bright six year olds, entering school with fresh hope. Certainly we assume they are early drop outs and have difficulty seeing them as once diligent high school or even college students, whose studies and exams have led them to the wilderness of street living.

Yet half of our street people have Grade 10 education or more - what a lot of education we are casting away into the street! Moreover, contrary to the image of street people as social misfits all the way, half liked school.

Ruth Morris and Colleen Heffren

Among those who felt positive and grateful for the education they had had was Phillip, an older native person:

> "I went to school for ten years, working off and on. I finished Grade 4. I liked school, only left because I had to work and the family needed my help. I can read some, and more could have helped me find a life work."

Donald, a young, unemployed, white Canadian said:

> "I learned what was going on in the world from school. I felt good about myself there."

Most of those who enjoyed school had to leave because of a variety of life pressures:

> "I finished Grade 11 with honours. I liked school. I left because I had to leave home, and couldn't afford to stay in school."

> "There was a teachers' strike, so I couldn't complete Grade 10. So I left, three-fourths through. I needed to help Mom support the family anyway."

> "I liked school some, but I had to drop out in Grade 10 because the family moved and left me on my own. I ended up on the street."

> "Grade 12 was almost finished, and I enjoyed it, but I left because of home problems in my foster home. School made me feel I was doing something with my life and being somebody."

A particularly poignant form of pressure came when parents actually pressured children to leave. Rob described his school experience:

> "I quit in Grade 10 because my stepfather was jealous and pressured me to get out and make a living. I was the valedictorian and made the speech in 8th grade. But he made fun of my accomplishments, so I began drinking

with him. School did expose me to the world of knowledge. Without it, I wouldn't be where I am now."

There is no irony in Rob's speaking of where he is now. This native has given much to his people and to the world and, incidentally, succeeded in getting out of the hostel/street world shortly after our interview with him. He spoke movingly of a teacher who contributed significantly, not only to his life but to many other native children's development:

> "One of the teachers who influenced me early was in Grade 7. He was very progressive, and taught me how to search for knowledge. You don't have to go to school to get knowledge. School forces you, but the pursuit of knowledge is anywhere. University teaches you how to pursue knowledge on your own.
>
> This teacher understood a lot about psychology. He taught us chess, and motivated us to read books. Within that year, I learned so much; because I wanted to play chess. He had us all reading books and playing chess and learning and asking questions. He also told us stories of our heritage."

Such inspired teachers are of course rare in any of our lives. Another group of street people had very mixed reactions to school. They liked some parts of it but ran into conflicts or problems with other parts:

> "Got to Grade 10. I liked it earlier, but not later. One teacher didn't like me and bugged me. Then I got in trouble with the police. But I liked math, and I wanted to finish and study robotics. I'm going part time now. I met some good people through school."

> "I finished Grade 10 and liked it. I done Grade 11 but failed. The demand for seats is such you can only come back for special reasons. I'd had enough and wanted to get to work anyway. I didn't know it was important. It was like a torture. But it was 80% positive, I just wasn't

giving it everything I have. Sports kept me in it for awhile - I got good marks in the subjects I liked."

This ambivalence to the point of inconsistency marked several of our conversations. Garth, a native alcoholic remembers this:

"I left during Grade 11; it was nice. I flunked Grade 5. I was more interested in sports. I left because I was already drinking, skipping school, and having trouble with the police. I wish I had had machine shop, auto mechanics, and carpentry. At that age, I didn't see my drinking as a problem."

Ken showed an amazing ability to gain positive stimulation from a very destructive start:

"The teachers took me out in kindergarten. They said I could not learn. Having no school gave me regret over lost possibilities, but it also increased the desire to learn for myself."

One group disliked school, did badly, and left early:

"I hated school. The only two areas I enjoyed with a passion were math and shops. School had little effect on me. I learned more on the street. If I had kids I wouldn't send them to school, but to the street. They would get more out of it."
"I was scared when I was little. I was afraid to ask to go to the washroom, and sometimes I wet myself. It was awful in school. I was not a great scholar."

"I never liked school, just finished Grade 2. I taught myself most of what I do know in institutions. Being shipped around from institution to institution, I didn't have time to learn much, or else fights broke out. I was a slow learner, and public schools were pushing to grind you on, but I kept flunking. Pressure from my parents and from the school made me feel bad."

These street people, so disillusioned with school, felt that the harsh realism of the street or of institutions taught them more of what they have needed in life. Or, perhaps, their disillusionment is with the things life itself has offered them!

Josh, a large native whom we met on a street corner, had something to say about his experiences of school as a native person:

> "I finished Grade 8, but I didn't like it. I left at sixteen, as soon as I was free to go. I wasn't good in math or French, but if they had taught me our native tongues! They didn't respect me, and where I came from."

A significant group of street people showed evidence of the ability to perform well, either by going further in school, getting scholastic recognition in some form, or by the general tenor of their interviews. They tended to blame their dislike of school on its regimented approach and its lack of creativity. Mark put it this way:

> "When in school, I was too creative for the confinement. It had a bad effect on me, because I was always a joker, and got the strap which made me more rebellious. I hated society, and wanted steel-toed shoes and greasy hair. It was a Catholic school, and my parents were very religious. I would like to go back now to better myself."

Jake had a sense of humour about his own inconsistency:

> "When I was sixteen, I left school because I was too rebellious. I don't know why, because I ended up joining the army!
>
> I was bored, felt school very irrelevant, and now wish I had gone further. I played the clown, and the only effect was to make me a little more stubborn. I was the highest math student in Grade 10."

Brant was not unduly modest, but his words echo those of many gifted students we have spoken with in other contexts:

"I was bored to death in school. If they had a school like Subway Stop (alternative school), I would have done well. It gives you the same credits, but you are allowed to work at your own speed. It's for highly intelligent people. In a typical school, the first three months review the last year. I have perfect recall, and a photographic memory, and get bored to death. I got lots of bad reports for my attitude and for not attending classes. But I could get 98% after the first three months without attending, because it was all repetition. I like to read the encyclopedia for fun."

Dick, on the other hand, stressed the regimentation in his own way:

"I hated school from day one till I quit in Grade 11. Regimentation! Everybody had to be doing exactly the same thing at the same speed. You didn't learn useful things, either.

At the end, I finally had one choice: whether to read *The Fifth Business* or *Catcher in the Rye*. I'd probably have done a lot better without school."

Tar went a little further than most, but still had no kind words for his schooling experience:

"School had nothing to offer as far as education. In a personal context, my parents taught me to be an independent thinker, while school taught me to fit in. I tolerated school to the end of Grade 13, but decided not to go to University. School brainwashed me."

Tar's independent character made one doubt that school had brainwashed him very far!

Jerry echoed some of the themes of others who disliked the rigidity of school, but added his own experiences:

> "I finished Grade 9. I didn't like it - it was too stifling. I did correspondence courses for a while, and found that really good. I could write five lessons on native people, could picture what the white man did. I wrote down how I was anti-system, and got nineties! It boosted my ego. But in general, I resisted regimentation. I can't sit in a class with thirty other people with the teacher in front writing on the chalkboard:
>
> 'Copy this down.'
>
> Then he hands out a sign 'Go' and doesn't care whether you live, die, pass, or fail, so long as he gets his paycheque. But there are some good teachers.
>
> Some of my anti-authoritarianism came from there; I have a lot of anger. I tried alternative schools, but they didn't work for me, because I needed some structure."

Jerry was able to own up to his own role in the mismatch between him and formal education. Yet, one can't help but regret seeing this bright and sensitive boy drifting, or wishing the school had managed to make the social connection for him which his family was unable to do.

School does not appear to be a prime villain in the lives of most street people, but neither does it seem to have been a very positive connection, except in rare instances. For the most part, school and the street people were like ships passing in the night.

2. Work

"Street people are lazy bums who don't want to work." But their lives contradicted this myth. There is wistful longing in their eyes when they speak of even the low paid, day to day, walking-in-the-rain or heavy labour casual jobs. In fact, as we shall hear from their accounts, the search for even the humblest jobs occupies the energies of many of them, day-in and day-out. As we saw earlier, about one-third placed a good job high in their dream list. Nevertheless, some of them do get discouraged and, more or less, drop out of the difficult competition for jobs:

> "I've done everything, but I'm not really trying anymore. It's a lack of willpower. I'm so depressed being fired for homosexuality, my criminal record, doing things I shouldn't do, but never seem able to change."

These words were from a chronically institutionalized man whose life shifted back and forth monotonously between the streets and institutions.

Charlie, on the other hand, was a native person, who had experienced a total breakdown after the breakup of his family:

> "After I lost my family and had the breakdown, I just gave it up. I had too many physical and emtional problems. I gave up wanting to work at all."

Just two people we spoke with reported no work history at all. One was Jerry, our youngest interviewee, who expressed a variety of reasons, from antagonism to government so that he didn't want to pay taxes, to lack of ability to get a job with little education and no experience. The other was Theo, who at thirty-seven, said:

> "I have NO work history. I've pumped gas, done a few manual things, but for a real job, you need experience, and all I have is institutions. But I am still trying to get off the street."

Looking back over his thirty years of struggling between street and institutions, this is a fairly amazing statement. He is still trying to escape the tentacles that hold him where he is.

STREET PEOPLE SPEAK

A number report a life coloured by all the occasional jobs they are able to obtain:

> "I've worked maybe a third of the time occasional labour, whatever I can get. I load trucks and do packing, more and more as the weather warms up."

> "I do odd jobs, whatever they want. The last two years, steady! You don't get much money. Once down here, you are stuck here."

> "There are no jobs without experience. I finished a course in architectural drafting, but I can't afford the five years training with no pay to get in, though I'd love to do the work. I do flyers and labour when I feel up to it for temporary work. My physical disability (leg injury in war) limits me."

This variation on the old Catch 22 could at least theoretically be breached by a kindly benefactor. But the loss of health described by many is an unsolvable barrier, as is discrimination against people with certain conditions:

> "I did welding, baking and driving for three years, till they found out I was epileptic. I will still work at anything they let me do. I have a college education, but I am doing casual jobs. I'm on partial medical disability now."

> "Because of the injury to my hands, I can't work now. I never received any compensation for these injuries, though they did happen on the job. I also have a bad leg."

> "The thing that bothers me most are my health and not being able to work. I am so used to working. Volunteering here enables me to see people worse off than I am. I worked till six months ago, even with cancer, emphysema, and two heart attacks, and now my broken foot keeps me from it."

This interview brings up two important topics. One is the indomitable desire to work in this man, as in many people we saw. The other is the important part volunteer work plays in the lives of some of the street people we talked with:

> "I am a native person, and I am proud to do volunteer work with my own people at the native centre. We have to support one another, as the white people certainly won't do much for us."

Finally, there is the tragic way in which the present job market punishes small errors;

> "The recession has contributed a lot to my situation. Since I was fired, they have cut down the people working there to a fraction of what they had then. The majority of my troubles are my own fault, but for 19 years here, I never had a problem. I worked two jobs when I first came to Canada to get established. Sure I made a mistake, but after 19 years of hard work and doing everything right, there should be some way I can retrieve myself from one mistake."

Of all the people we interviewed, 40% had worked nine or more years, and over half had worked some 75-100% of their adult life. Clearly, although the world of well-paid, secure jobs is, at present, closed to them, work plays an important part in their lives, and their labour contributed far more to our maintenance than we often are aware.

3. Agencies

A number of agencies exist in part or entirely to serve street people. So, it was interesting and valuable to get their viewpoint as consumers whose views and preferences were important.

As we had expected, government services such as welfare hostels were more criticized than appreciated. In contrast, drop-ins got much more appreciation. Yet, the most striking factor was that about half the street people had nothing good or bad to say about these agencies. They either hesitated to speak frankly about the powers on which they depend for their continued survivial, or perhaps, the realities of cold, wind, hunger, rain and danger on the street occupied their minds more. The other half did comment and had a good deal to say.

Hostels come in for a lot of criticism because they are doing a job with built in pressure for non-excellence. If we were willing to foot the real bill, there wouldn't be any hostels because there would be enough economical, long term housing for everybody. So with low per-diem funding, the hostels are under pressure to cram many people into few spaces. As well, low paid staff are told to shorten their hours in order to cut costs. As one, very fair-minded street person put it:

> "There's lots of good to hostels, but still they are a necessary evil, sleeping 500 men. It's an awful place to spend any length of time. And some of the workers are worked very hard."

In spite of these difficulties, some hostels evoked positive comments. The family hostels and especially the Good Shepherd Refuge were appreciated for their spirit of caring, as well as their specific supports:

> "The Good Shepherd Refuge has clean pajamas EVERY NIGHT! Very nice."

> "The Brothers (same place) is very good, they have good meals, and really care for you."

> "The family hostel people have been remarkably understanding of our position."

In fact, there were many tributes to the Brothers, except one person warned us how hard it is to get in:

> "The Good Shepherd is the Holiday Inn of the street: it's a lottery to get in, and you win the clean pjs and all.

Ruth Morris and Colleen Heffren

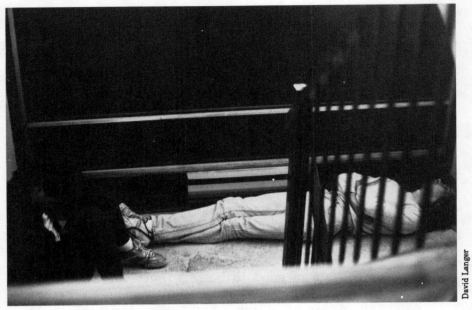

Stairwells of apartment buildings are often found by those desperate for shelter.

STREET PEOPLE SPEAK

Toronto's bus shelters offer minimal rest and protection for street people.

Ruth Morris and Colleen Heffren

They're all clean in exactly the same way, so you can't tell the real down and outs from just plain down and outs, which is good.

But to get in, you line up at the back door. First they take over fifties who stayed there last night, then over forties, then over thirties, then the new ones draw for beds. By the time you lose, it's too late for all but the worst places."

Hostels are subject to both general and specific complaints. A number of the people on the street explained graphically just why they didn't use hostels except in the direst of circumstances:

"I don't use hostels. I was in an emergency one recently because I was so hungry. The places are too dirty, real hell holes, and too many people drunk."

"I don't use hostels - I'd rather sleep outside. You get sick in hostels; there is a concentration of sick people. People vomit and wet on beds, have colds and other bugs. Some get in fights. I'd rather buy my own food than eat their white bread. But in winter I usually have to use hostels."

Several people commented that hostels were dangerous places, where it was too easy to meet a drunk with a knife or other forms of aggression:

"I've been attacked about twenty times in the past five years in hostels, and been threatened one hundred times; young punks, trying to run the hostels."

Others commented on the general quality of hostels:

"Hostels are mediocre: just 'another job for those people'."

"Hostels are only a flophouse. They don't really help you. They take your money if you want a place to stay and abide by their regulations, and if you don't like it, hit the road..."

STREET PEOPLE SPEAK

Most of the natives we talked with did not use hostels and they gave us a variety of explanations. Some preferred the relative quiet and freedom of the street. One suggested it was discrimination:

> "Indians don't go in hostels. They give you a hard time, call you a — bum."

A more specific complaint about hostels was their hours. One man commented on the closing hours, along with some other concerns:

> "There's too much hassle in hostels. If you aren't there by a certain time, you don't get in. For Good Shepherd it's 7; Sally Ann 9:30; Dixon Hall 10; and Seaton House, 11. I wouldn't send my friends to hostels - they are too dirty."

If all this sounds like beggars trying to be choosers, it raises the question of whether beggars should not be entitled to some preferences and judgments of their lives, too. It has been said that the quality of a society can be judged by the state of its prisons. It may also be judged by the facilities it offers to its poorest and most helpless groups.

Just as early closing hours were a problem for some, early ejection caused serious money problems for many:

> "Hostels could improve - kicking guys out at 7:30 a.m. in winter. What about older fellows, keeping them in till 9 a.m.? They can't work, and the malls aren't even open. Some of them just crouch and rock on street heating vents. It's not necessary for us younger guys, we can take it, but there should be some compassion for the older ones."

> "My biggest complaint is the 'hostilities'. Why should we be turned out seven days a week at 6:30 or 7 a.m.? Saturday and Sunday there's no way to find work, and

we are not allowed back for hours. We are forced to walk the streets.

Then there is the two week limit. It is a Catch 22, because the other hostels are closed and full when you have to leave one because your two weeks is up. And those paper towels they sell you for fifteen cents at the Sally Ann for showers - have you ever tried wiping your whole body with a paper towel! And charging people who have nothing for it, too.

Another problem is their hours - you can't have a shift job and sleep in a hostel. They don't accpet the idea; they have no beds in the day. And when you are signed up for a two week period, you can't miss a night for work or anything else, or you won't be allowed back for three months!"

Seaton House, partly because it is such a large, impersonal facility serving too many people at once, came in for a lot of criticism. It should be remembered that without Seaton House's many beds, many more people would be sleeping directly on the streets. At the same time, one may ask whether some of the following complaints could be addressed:

"Seaton's the worst hostel in town, lots of people get hurt there. We call it 'coakroach hotel'."

"Seaton House, the 'Bon Ami Hotel', is operated as BS. They do have a good facility, if they had good people who cared. It's supposed to be run by government personnel, but the couldn't give a damn. They are there to put in their time and make their money and get out."

A particularly pathetic man in a leather jacket with no seams, dirty t-shirt and totally destitute appearance observed:

"I'm trying to survive as best I can by staying at different places. I can't stay at Seaton House. It's a common body (sic) house and people rip everything off your belongings."

STREET PEOPLE SPEAK

Some people, even in such dire straits, managed to understand the problems of those working in the hostels:

"Seaton House (the Ranch, because you feel like cattle) is pretty awful. You can understand the staff's 'no give a hoot' attitude, because they handle hundreds of people a night. But they have to have compassion, even though it's hard for them to keep tuned to it."

Rounding out the list of hostel criticisms, two people suumed up the general perspectives of most:

"The Brothers are doing a good job, and Fred Victor was. Seaton House, my overall feeling is not to go if I have a choice, but they do feed you."

"Fred Victor staff were excellent, Dixon Hall O.K. As for Seaton House, I'd rather live in a tree. Scott Mission are great people. You don't have to be anybody to be welcomed there."

Jack, a sophisticated young man not long on the street, had a number of useful insights. He suggested improving the security of the hostels and respecting the needs of those who find shift jobs. Small is beautiful is a good theme which gets at the root of many of the problems. Of course, the whole hostel system exists because we don't care to provide enough really small, individualized housing for low income people.

John Jagt, the manager for Metro's hostel system, pointed out some of the challenges and also the seriousness with which hostels are trying to plug an increasingly large gap in our housing:

"Toronto has the best hostel situation in all of Canada: Seaton, All Saints, Sally Ann, Good Shepherd. In Calgary and Vancouver, there is only one place."

But without disputing that our hostel system is superior to most and that we have increased our commitment to it enormously, the comments of our street people raise serious questions. Do the nature of hostels prevent them from being part of the solution, and does the spirit of caring penetrate to most of the hostels? The starkly different comments about Good Shepherd and most of the other hostels suggest that it is more than the clean pajamas. The men and women in hostels are just as perceptive about the difference in staff as any other consumer group. Yet it is clear that the pressures of doing a low status service for a low status group, in a situtation which strongly calls for more basic solutions, is so hard on staff that it is a miracle Good Shepherd manages to transcend it. As Brad Lennon, the Minister of All Saints Church which has pioneerred in both emergency housing and long term solutions, observed:

> "This is the most heavily serviced area in Canada. The system won't work. The problem is a shortage of housing, not services. In our random survey in '81, NOT ONE PERSON WANTED TO BE IN HOSTEL. They preferred a room of their own, or an apartment. They chose the park bench over hostels, for privacy. They have no real choices, because they have no good options. People can't get out. The market system keeps people out, then says 'They can get out if they try', but it's not true."

Turning from hostels to welfare is a logical step, for welfare exists to fill the other critical gap for street people - lack of money. A surprising number of street people did appreciate the existence of welfare. Homeless familes found welfare more understanding and supportive than single men. But one unemployed young black observed:

> "Welfare and places like that get more abuse than they should. Some are real complaints, but a lot of the welfare people are trying their best; they just have to go by the books. They try to be fair."

A young homeless father described welfare as "very helpful, most helpful," while a homeless mother said, "Welfare has helped me out a lot - they bought me a stroller." Nonetheless, welfare came in for a number of complaints:

> "Before I came here I got $280 a month welfare, and owed a rent of $160 a month. It just isn't enough, I was always hungry. I lived on a cup of tea and two pieces of toast most days, and when I was specially hungry I would go to Scotts."

Another regulation that caused problems was the limit on extra money to get a room. Both the limit of fourteen days to find such a place and the waiting period of six months before you could try again if you failed came in for criticism. But the most severe criticism was one of attitude. Tony, an alcoholic who spent years struggling to get out of the system, observed:

> "Welfare bugs me. For the little amount of money they give you, they sure put you through a wringer."

Others made similar comments:

> "Welfare is dehumanizing, it seems to want to keep you going round and round. They don't really care. 'Your cheque is in the mail, but you aren't entitled to it because you don't have residence.' I had to go fifteen miles on the bus, to be told it was mailed. I waited so long, I had to miss a job appointment. When she told me it was already mailed I said I had a job appointment in just twenty minutes now. 'Well, you might make it anyway', she said, 'And besides, I don't like your attitude!"

> "We should start over again on the whole welfare system. Welfare workers look down on you. 'I'm making 30,000 a year and you're just a bum, so why should I help you,' is their attitude. Then they are so limited in where you can go, what you can do. If you need glasses, you have to go to the other end of the city, and walk there because there are no bus tickets, and then you have to wait three

weeks for the glasses. But FBA is much better. It's enough to get you just above the poverty level and they don't hassle you."

FBA or Family Benefits Assistance is a higher level of assistance available to those the system considers more "worthy poor". The fact that the same people can move back and forth between the two forms of assistance illustrates its inconsistency as well as its "judgment-oriented" approach. The whole system is currently under review and the recommendation of many groups is to undo and revise the entire system.

Street people saw differences in the attitudes of many groups that are there to "serve" them. Some were seen as just in it for the money:

"They are driving $20,000 cars with air conditioners and stereos: Toyotas, Datsuns, Capris, and brand new vans every two years."

While some of this may be exaggerated, it illustrates the problem of relatively wide income gaps between people on the street and those who attempt to assist them. A more general problem of feeling that they are treated as grist for the social workers' mill pervades some of the street people's comments:

"Children's Aid are like a bunch of kids out of school trying to analyze people's lives through a textbook. They are hypocritical and don't know what they are doing."

"Counsellors refer you to different agencies, and you go round in circles. Agencies pass the buck, and do as little as possible for you. The only thing that keeps me going is my faith."

"Immigration? I don't find them friendly. If they were in my situation, they would understand it is not easy to survive. They make all kinds of money, and they don't give us the right to eat. If they send me back home, I would be in jail the rest of my life."

This moving comment by a refuge at least makes one smile with his understatement about not finding immigration friendly!

One of the native people we interviewed didn't find the police very friendly:

"The police hit me with billyclubs on the forehead just for sleeping in the park (pointing to the bloody crevasses on his forehead and nose). The police give Indians most of the scars you see on us. Fourteen Division is a rough outfit."

A particularly poignant cry from the heart came from Will, a weary and somewhat disillusioned young man:

"I'm not entitled to things as I would be in a natural society. With the monetary system, once you're down, it's hard to get up. I don't pay taxes, as I won't work for this government. I won't work for this country and pay taxes because we are not doing a good enough job with people. You help an animal, but you watch people go down. Street people are chilled to their bones, and social workers ask these questions 10,000 times."

An equally poignant comment came from Clem, a native person who listed several agencies that he felt did help, then added wistfully:

"I wish they would give me more time to talk, and listen to me sometimes."

Yet street people had some good words to say about services. Even in the midst of their desperate lives, they found time to be grateful for those they could see directy helping them. It is not surprising, when one thinks of about it, that drop-ins got more favourable mentions than hostels. Drop-ins, by their very nature, are open-ended where there is a little more time for that "listening" Clem longed for. Hostels and welfare are, by definition, dealing with more concrete services, such as beds and money. Public health, community centres, and foodbanks all got some appreciation. However, foodbanks, for the most part, touch street people only indirectly, for they lack cooking facilities. Several people commented favourable on the Fred Victor Mission, and All Saints Church's Open Door and Friendship Centre. They appreciated the forty cent sandwiches and the spirit behind them. Older street people appreciated the services of a seniors drop-in called the Good Neighbours Club. As one awed senior observed:

> "They even let you wash your clothes sometimes!"

St. Stephen's Caring Corner drop-in, where we did some of our interviewing, also got some appreciative comments. But if we were to take a popularity poll of the most appreciated service, there is little doubt that the Scott Mission would be a clear winner, with Good Shepherd Refuge a strong second. Of the many who made warm, deeply appreciative comments about Scott, two people summed up the essential points clearest. Tony, a chronic alcoholic on the road toward rehabilitation, noted:

> "The Scott Mission are wonderful. There should be more places like them. Without them, there would be a lot more hungry people: they CARE. They will go out of their way to help you in any way they possibly can."

Ned, a native alcoholic critical of many of the services, said:

> "The Scott Mission is good. They won't refuse you if you are a little drunk. They even give you bag lunches. They do what they can. Just because they have suits on, and we come in dirty old clothes doesn't mean they are going to kick you out. They will joke with you when they sense you are down, and try to cheer you up."

Finally, Rob in reporting on experiences with agencies in his life demonstrated a certain kind of cold clear assessment:

> "On the surface, they are cold, but once you get to know them and make friends, they're O.K. I had one confrontation with a woman in —. She said some remarkable things - told me to go back to the reservation. This was our first day here, and she asked me why we came to take a vacation on government expense."

Rob actually managed to laugh in a relaxed and good-natured way as he continued his story:

> "I gave her a brief history of the proclamation of the treaties and native history generally. But a lot of people are too down; they don't fight back. I went to the other social workers and they had a meeting about it and she apologized, not too willingly. But I've had a chance to talk with her since, and she is different now; sees me as a person. She got burnt out with overwork and lost perspective. As a professional, she never should have, not those kind of remarks. But we're friends now."

Rob certainly put it all together - standing up for principles against oppression, dealing with it individually and on a system level, understanding the causes and seeking individual reconciliaton in the end.

4. How You See Us

We asked street people how they felt about the reactions of the average person on the street to them. Their responses were a kaleidoscope of reactions, reminding one of the diversity of the group called "street people". A number commented on a sense of coldness and distance, of social separation:

> "Toronto is a cold city. I'm the same person as if I was employed, but people don't respect me. This whole area has a stigma."

> "Toronto is a very cold city compared to the East, where I come from."

"People make me feel like a bum. Not anything they said, they didn't say anything. But if they saw me coming, they would try to ignore me, or even cross the street. I have never done that to anybody."

"Everyone just seems to come and go without really taking notice."

A native commented on the sense of neglect tied to this social aloofness:

"I feel anger. People used to be friendlier. Everyone seems to ignore us. People let other people die on the streets. Too many people are dying, and the others are not looked after."

One of the unemployed young men commented differently:

"They do have a tendency on occasion to turn their heads - it doesn't bother me. I sort of take the general attitude that they have their lives, and I just go about mine."

Tom, a native alcoholic, observed:

"They smile at you when you are stemming; or they tell you 'fuck off, you fucking bum'. Sometimes they throw the money on the sidewalk, and you have to smile and pick it up and keep going. Sometimes they treat you like dirt. But mostly there is a lack of real communication. They sometimes give you money or food, but they never know you."

One man summed up the sense of separation with its overtones of rejection which pervaded the comments of this whole group:

"We don't fit in with the rest of society. You can tell that when you go uptown - segregated groups. They look down on us. They seem to ignore us like we are nonexistent. Maybe that's better than their paying attention, the kind of attention they do pay. Only security guards and police pay attention. They're on the lookout for you all the time. You feel like you are imposing when you go to their stores, or anywhere they hang around."

Len summed up the defeated apathy of those who felt this icy wall of indifference and contempt:
"I move out of the way."

Another group expressed ambivalence and often a whole variety of feelings in their comments. Young Jerry was one of them:

"I don't mind them. I hate rush hour though - you see all the people rushing around, going nowhere. I used to more radical. When I dressed punk, people looked at me, yelled at me, and beat me up. What the heck is the point - I never did anything to them. But there are some generous people out there, too."

Trent, a native alcoholic, sensed the feeling of helplessness of many passersby:

"They look at you like you are really dumb. They wanna help, but they can't."

Another native person expessed some yearning for more of a connection:

"I don't feel anger, but I feel they could help more. They could stop and at least try to be polite when I stop to try to talk to them. And sometimes they get very abusive."

Nat, a mentally ill person, expressed both ambivalence and the sense of distance and unreality to the contacts between our worlds:

"It'a all a game. People smile at you and spit at you. They seem to me like a scene someone puts before me, to no purpose."

Finally, one young man expressed the way we look to them in this fashion:

> "There are so many different kinds of people. There is a lot of greed. I would die before I would become like that. People who pass us by are just as cold as a lot of people who konk others on the head. The don't konk people on the head; they just take away their livelihood - and they're STILL not pleased with their own lives, still complaining."

From negative tinted ambivalence, it is a small step to the bitterly angry resonses of a number of the street people:

> "I get to feeling aggressive with the way people sneer at me, like I was a bug out of the sewer."

> "I feel like a piece of garbage when I'm on the street among averge people. I feel angry if people don't respond to me, at least answer when I say hello. I feel like lashing out at them physically."

> "They respond with no respect. I built up an attitude where if I saw a person wouldn't move, I would bump right into them. It frustrates me."

> "They treat me like they think the worst of me. The real passersby are the fumes from the cars."

Another person felt the injustice of their struggle to survive, and the small returns they got for it compared to the fortunate lot of many others in Toronto:

> "It bugs me seeing young punks who don't know how to tie their shoelaces talking about buying big homes; but we who work hard just to survive, don't have anything."

A very interesting group expressed varying kinds of pity for us and a sense that they knew something we were missing:

"Everyone is in their little cliques, and it is hard to cross over. In Vancouver, it is easier to go from rich to poor. Here I find more entrenched racism, much more than they let on. I know the difference! I'm the one (waving his Indian braid) who goes looking for apartments. A lot of people haven't grown from their racism."

Another native person observed philosophically:

"Sometimes I feel sorry for them - there is nothing I can do about it; it is their life."

An ex-mental patient also felt a sense of sympathy for the apparent "haves" he met on the street:

"They seem sad. They seem to be looking for something better: which makes sense?"
An older man commented with more bitterness:

"They look at you as if you're dirty, but I don't mind because I know they're as much dirt as I am. And the kind of dirt on them can't wash off, but the dirt on me you CAN wash off."

A young woman looking at her generation from the vantage point of a broken marriage with young children on her hands noted:

"A lot of my community are missing something, though I don't mean to put them down. But they are smiling at you, while they are so empty. People my age try to be what they are not. There is so much more to life than discos. I don't want to kill time. We have a saying in my home country: 'Life is only three days, and two of them are already gone.'"

Two men summed up a lot of street wisdom in their comments on the general public. Neil, a young husband struggling with an unhoused family to support, exclaimed:

"Before I was in this position, I would have called anyone on welfare a lazy bum. Now that I have gone through it myself, I realize how easily it can happen. But you can't believe it can ever happen to you."

At this point, I started to ask him if he were ever to recover his position, whether he would remember. But he cut in before I finished the question, saw where I was going, and answered emphatically: "No, I will NEVER FORGET this. I won't ever go back to not understanding how easy it is to be in trouble and need help, and have the world turn its back on you."

To us, the most haunting of comments came from Tom, who had spent years on the street, and who described his exact sensations in this way:

"They look at you like "HUH, who is this guy?" They don't want any part of you, like you are dirt.

Did you ever watch a streetcar go by, and see the whole streetcar look at you with disgust? I have been on that corner, and seen those looks. They should think, 'Thank God, through the grace of God, I am not there.' Because the same thing could happen to them.

When I was fourteen or fifteen, I used to go by Queen and Sherbourne, and think, 'I'll never be there'. And I ended up there for two and a half years!"

CHAPTER FIVE: MESSAGE

Tell Toronto This!

STREET PEOPLE
By Rob Keehn

*There are people destined - destined to wander
To roam through this world - all alone,
To touch other lives only briefly,
Then in solitude - keep movin' on.*

*Not for them is the home - home and the family
Or the loves that keep most of us warm...*

*Their weakness and pain is what keeps them alive,
And they wish, God they wish, that they could be strong.*

Ruth Morris and Colleen Heffren

*They keep searchin for something, something that's better,
But that better thing just never comes.
If they touch you, all I ask is that you treat them with kindness,
For they could be your daughters or sons,
For they could be YOUR daughters or sons.*

Rob Keehn's moving song makes a fitting introduction to this section. We looked forward to the end of each interview with a mixture of feelings. It was hard to walk away after people had shared with us so deeply, to say thank you and goodbye, and in many cases we did become friends and continued seeing them. But in every interview, we looked forward to the last question, for it was their chance, in a world which had been mostly deaf to them and their needs, finally to be heard. Their responses too, were almost invariably moving and exciting. Our last question was usually worded something like this:

> "We are writing this book to try to help people in Toronto understand people on the street better. If you could speak directly through the pages of our book to the people of Toronto, what would you say?"

We sorted the answers that came into a progressive series:

Thanks - for what you are doing

Anger

You don't listen

You don't respect us

It's rough on the street

It can happen to anyone!

STREET PEOPLE SPEAK

You don't understand

WE NEED HOUSING!

There is a logical sequence to this beginning with appreciation for the help being received and moving on to anger at the yawning abyss of neglected needs. The street people cry that we are NOT LISTENING. An important part of that failure to listen is our lack of respect for them, based on our belief that it can't happen to us, or that they got there because, somehow, they deserved it. From this, many of them conclude that we seem incapable of understanding, even when we make some effort to listen and show respect. And what is it that we don't understand? Simply, that they NEED HOUSING!

THANKS — FOR WHAT YOU ARE DOING

Even in the difficulty of their position, some of our street people managed to think of our vantage point and to express appreciation for the gestures we are making. Stan, an older man who has been reduced to street life by a combination of widowhood, old age, and gradually increased drinking, said:

> "The programs you give to us are good. People do think about us. I don't think we had some of those programs twenty years ago."

An ex-mental patient actually remembered to be grateful for welfare, so often everyone's favourite whipping-boy from both ends:

> "Thank you for your governmental donations and concern through the welfare department."

An absolutely unique and very moving message came from another ex-mental patient. From the heart of his own need, to the need which is in every one of us:

> "Tell them - that they are loved."

Ruth Morris and Colleen Heffren
ANGER

At the opposite pole, others lashed out in general anger. A gentle, good-humoured old man astonished us after an interview full of benign apathy with these closing words:

> "I'd like to see the rich exterminated, because they hold the keys to the lives of the poor. It's their attitude that makes me so angry!"

An unemployed youth compressed the breakdown of all his dreams into these words:

> "This city is horrible. The police are corrupt. No one will do anything to help others; people aren't welcome. The jobs are sham jobs. You can fill out job applications all day, and not get a job. I've been freezing all day in winter, and nobody cares."

Not surprisingly, those suffering from the double bind of race prejudice and anti-street prejudice tended to be especially bitter. A black immigrant observed:

> "Why let people come here, and then not enable them to work and be a part of society? There's a lot of racist b.s. from people."

Another black man who was native to Toronto, well educated, and unemployed at thirty-two, with a family to support, observed angrily:

> "People don't care about other people. The system is rotten. The Landlord and Tenant Act allows rents too high, and there's no place for us to live!"

A single parent mother, left by her husband and his family to look after their children, with no home and no income, expressed her own philosophy of letting nature take its course in getting back at those who hurt others:

STREET PEOPLE SPEAK

"Some of my friends think I should be trying to get back at my husband and his family, but I don't want to. We have a saying in my culture, 'Every pig has its Christmas.' You see, we have a roasted pig for Christmas every year; so it's a way of saying: 'Don't worry, if you deserve it, you'll get yours.' Let life take its course, I don't need to get back."

YOU DON'T LISTEN

A major reason for anger is the sense that you are not being listened to. A number of street people expressed this feeling. One advised us to:

"Stop sticking your noses in the air when you're asked for money."

With more patience, another said:

"Not all street people are bad. I'd like to see more people who need help get it. Most people turn their head, and say they can't help."

A native person urged:

"Tell them to CARE MORE. To listen to us when we talk, and not to ignore us, or laugh at us."

Tim was cynical in his advice to us:

"I think you are wasting your time, because THEY'RE NEVER GOING TO CHANGE. They like it the way it is. They feel we are down here because we deserve it; because we are lazy and drunks, the bottom of the barrel."

This challenge to the sensitivity of our readers and our city was echoed in even more poignant terms by Clyde, who with an injured back and no family support, struggled to survive on the streets:

"People are aware of the situation. Some people do their best, some would like to, but the majority say, 'Look after your own problems, up yours!'"

YOU DON'T RESPECT US

This sense that they are not accepted by us permeates many of the interviews. The native people are keenly aware of this, to the point where some of them don't even bother to mention it. Two who did put it this way:

"They wouldn't listen to me, anyway. But I wish they would be polite at least, and not laugh at me."

"I'd like to be given respect, and the dignity of my person."

Andy, who made the first comment, is a shrivelled, wornout, native who looks in his fifties, yet is in his thirties. Can we meet the challenge of showing real respect to him?

A young unemployed Canadian white man who had also experienced social rejection put his message this way:

"Everything that is living is life. You have to treat it with respect, and protect it, not destroy it."

Mark spelled it out in the most depth for us:

"I would tell 90% of them that they are WRONG for putting themselves higher than others, and criticizing them. They are working class, and they can't accept the people lower than them. They want to prosecute something they don't understand.

The struggling people on the street are trying even harder than the ones criticizing."

STREET PEOPLE SPEAK
IT'S ROUGH ON THE STREET

One of the most important things street people don't feel we understand is how rough it is on the street. If we did, how could we show so little respect to them? How could we fail to admire their courage in surviving in such arduous conditions? How could we fail to listen to their pleas for help in housing? The first misconception we need to get rid of is that street life or welfare existence is fun, or that people choose it just for the pleasure of living off of us:

> "It's awful being poor, and there are a lot of awfully poor people on the street."

> "It's not a bed of roses out there. People are in a dreamland, thinking we want to be here. Some people just don't care about us."

> "Welfare is a jail. People come there, hoping to get a break, but it's a vicious circle, and once you are caught, it's very hard to get out of it."

> "There is no LIFE on the streets. It is so much better to be self sufficient, to have some sort of job, and home, and friends. You miss all those things desperately, on the street."

There is also the sheer physical danger on the street:

> "I've seen everything in nine years, people getting killed. I'm used to it, and don't get scared anymore. If I could only get a place, I'd get a fulltime job."

But until this dishevelled person in tattered clothes gets a base to clean up and dress up, his chances at a job are nil, despite his good articulation and a very pleasant manner.

The final important point we don't understand is how the sheer struggle for survival saps people's strength:

"It's not nice to be living in the streets. But if you do, you have to get to know the ropes, just to survive. I survive, that is all, but that is a lot."

Bob left us with a fitting observation to conclude on the struggle to survive:

"Tell them what it is like to force myself to do everything while depressed and overtired, and knowing the MOST I can get out of it is mere physical survival. And what it is like to feel so totally alone against the world."

IT CAN HAPPEN TO ANYONE

"Tell them that we are no different from them: We are just not so lucky."

This theme is reiterated by many people in one form or another. Nellie, the single mother just quoted, tried to get across the idea that street people are just like us in this way:

"Sure, some people are lazy, but if they take a good look, most people are ashamed to ask for help. I don't want to come back actively to my community till I can come back with pride. People are NOT lazy, they just need temporary help. And it is very hard for most people to ask, without the extra burden of being blamed for it."

Young Brent was clear and eloquent:

"Tell them that people on the street are not that different from them. We have just had some tough breaks. Lots are just like you - no better, no worse. A lot of us are trying hard to get out of here, but don't have any success. Give us a break - Lord knows we could use it!"

A father in the family hostel summed up his advice:

"Save your money for a rainy day - it can happen to you! It can happen to ANYONE. There is a former cop in the

family residence - it's amazing who gets into it. There's a guy who was a graphics artist. One major reason for it all is the high cost of housing. If you are making $7 an hour, you just can't afford a place. The formula is: no place - no job - no haircut and suit - no job - no place."
Jim summed it all up this way:

"Tell them that we are human beings. We are just like everybody else, except that we don't have fancy homes, big cars, and good jobs. And it CAN HAPPEN TO YOU; it did to me.

I had it all: a three bedroom home in —, a family room with a fireplace, 1700 square feet, a wife, a daughter, a dog, a camper-trailer, $20,000 a year and an expense account. But they just figure we are stupid, and write us off."

YOU DON'T UNDERSTAND

When all is said and done, the most heartrending cries from the street are the almost despairing calls for understanding. Even when we listen a little, often we don't seem to them really to understand. Some doubt that we CAN understand without sharing their experience:

"I have been through it all, and you really have to experience it. I'm not saying 'Go out and live on the street,' because God help them, I hope they never do.

I don't think anybody ever could understand, but they can get an idea. But if you have been through it, you know. It's like so much in life; you have to experience it to understand."

A refugee echoed the earlier words of those who felt we don't understand that they don't CHOOSE to live this way:
"Nobody WANTS to come to the street. All people don't live the way you do. Many people are poor."

Ruth Morris and Colleen Heffren

Their right to work:

> "I would speak up about our lives. Any refugee should have the right to work and earn money, because they need to survive. They have a family to support back home, often. They suffer. It is all very difficult. Those who have families in Chile should have the right to work here, because their children need to eat."

The reality of their humanity:

> "I like everyone; I feel no resentment. I want everyone to be friends with me, and me with them. Tell Toronto how the street people REALLY live - our pain, sorrows, needs, and that we are REAL PEOPLE."

> "The street people of Toronto have a lot to offer. They need help to give it. Not everyone is on the street from their own doing. You don't cease to be people when you are kicked out. But the more years on the street, the worse their minds become. The more they get into bitters, drugs, etc., the less they can look for work. They are too exhausted. Sometimes it takes five years to get to you, sometimes five minutes. They need help and hope - more hope than help."

The reality of their suffering:

> "Everyone on the street has their own problems. If people could be more understanding - some have been through extremely rough times. It's not just coping with their families' rejection, but with themselves - loneliness from not liking yourself.

> The more people reject you, the harder it is for you to go on. This is why the guys binge bitters and do drugs; to get away from reality. The hardest part is trying to escape reality. Other people can make it a lot harder still. For

STREET PEOPLE SPEAK

me, I try to help other street people, and in doing it, I help myself. I have a degree in street psychiatry, from the streets."

A native person, dirty and unkempt, his face seamed, his nose bloody, challenged us with these words:

"I want them to understand that I feel pain. I'd like to have someone really love me, and people care about me."

A young, unemployed black man, in the midst of an otherwise fairly routine interview, brought us up with this thought:

"Which is better, intelligence or wisdom? Intelligence is what you are given, but wisdom is something that grows as time goes on. Who do you think has more wisdom: you or us?"

Who knows in that "last judgment" scene, what the answer to that query will be?

A native alcoholic summed up the reality of suffering in words we chose for the cover of this book:

"I want people to hear me,
And understand my pain.
I want to be a better person,
But I AM an important person, and a good one."

WE NEED HOUSING!

Person after person gave this simple message: WE NEED HOUSING! It ought to be obvious without their saying it, but we try to avoid the basic issue of the homeless by looking sideways, trying for root causes, therapy, punishment, or whatever. The homeless themselves are eloquent in sticking to the real point:

Ruth Morris and Colleen Heffren

"The housing situation is most important: you should be working on it till you can come up with the building programs you keep talking about, but don't seem to be DOING."

"Homeless people need housing. Most of these people are lonely. Make the streets safer for kids; more drop-in centres for kids where they can get support, and not end up here."

"I want a place to LIVE - that's the most part of it. I just want a place to live." (Repeated throughout the interview.)

Some people focussed on the dome, incuding one ex-mental patient who waxed poetic:

"It's clear that the sky is the limit,
The government won't help us at all:
The sky is the limit -
We are doomed, and domed!"

Others made briefer pleas:

"Just a room, I want to pay for a decent room."

"We're on the street, and we'd like to be off."

"The government should put out affordable housing."

"Don't live in Toronto. No reasonable accommodation for a reasonable price. If I'd realized, I never would have come here."

Tim, a chronically institutionalized man whose whole life had been spent between streets and institutions, still had room to dream of helping others:

"It feels bad here. If I had my way, I would go out and get an apartment building, and turn it into helping people."

But Rob summed up the plea for housing, challenging us with these words:

> "The message is so clear, but a lot of people don't even see it. Christian people often practice the formula, but not the substance. But we Ojibway do too. We are taught the whole world is our livingroom, and we need to live by that. You have to grow beyond the control of market economics and unthinking peer values. You need to realize your integrity is the ultimate. You have to make your own decision.
>
> Everybody has a right to shelter, because society can provide it for everybody, and everybody needs and deserves it. You have one person living in a home that can house 40, and 40 in a space that should house one. Inequality is the root of the problem. There is something wrong with us!"

Rob's words echo through the pages of this book, challenging us to look at the streets, as caring individuals, to listen to the voices of its men and women and to respond to them as human beings. It is for us to reach across the barriers to them, as they have to us, through the realities, the hopes and dreams, the fears and sorrows that they have shared with us here.

Next time you meet one, perhaps you will recognize in them someone you know through the pages of this book.

Ruth Morris and Colleen Heffren

Toronto's homeless have nothing to share and separate picnic benches in the Regent Park area to keep their isolation safe.

CHAPTER SIX: PROFILES

1. Mac, Child of the Working Class Poor

It is hard not to be bitter if you walk around in Mac's shoes. His unemployed father threw Mac out to get a job when Mac was only fifteen. Mac was the oldest of ten chidlren. The problems at home inhibited Mac at school. How could he concentrate when his father would hit the bottle, and then take it out on him? For the first couple of weeks after Mac was thrown out, scared and alone at fifteen, his mother was able to sneak him in to sleep in the basement. But then he was found out by his father and even this surreptitious shelter was denied him.

Mac has been homeless for 16 years, the most important years of his life. He worries about how little he has accomplished. He does the odd job, but poverty has been hard. He has gotten into trouble and gone to jail for theft and even robbery. He tries to keep a sense of purpose in his life by struggling to control his temper and to grow in maturity. But happiness is a stranger to him. Mac's life is very isolated, and he observes, "People look at me like a piece of skin."

Mac does have some contact with his Grandfather. His mother died of cancer two years ago and Mac feels even more severed from the family he barely knows now. Even his Grandad's relation to him is a mixed blessing. As welfare expects him to go way out to the suburban office near his Grandfather. Mac doesn't go, because he lives on the streets downtown, where he can also look for work.

Mac feels hardened towards life. "I've seen everything, even people getting killed - but I'm not afraid."

Mac goes on through life, whistling in the dark, dreaming of the fading hope of a fulltime job, a home with a wife and family. But he is caught in the vortex of his childhood's ejection, his lack of a base now, and the no job - no home dilemma.

2. Jerry, Rebel Child

Jerry is an affable youngster who seems a little older than his seventeen years. And no wonder, for three of them have been lived on the streets! Jerry comes from a thoroughly respectable upper middle class home. His mother is a phsychologist, his father a small businessman. Jerry was an only child till he was eight, when his brother was born. Though Jerry loves his brother, he feels his relations with his parents began to sour about the time his brother was added to the family. He is reluctant to criticize his parents and blames himself for some of the troubles.

"I always had problems in school; I just can't handle authority. Then I started dressing punk, with dyed hair and chains on my jacket. I gave my parents a hard time. We hurt each other a lot."

Jerry questions many things in the world. Even alternative schools were not altogether free enough for him. Finally, when he was fourteen, his father had had it. He packed Jerry into the car, took him to Children's Aid, and said, "We don't want him anymore."

When we asked Jerry what his mother thought about this, he said:
"I don't know. She was on a professional trip. I suppose she agreed, and that they had talked it over before sometime."

As to his current life, Jerry feels there aren't enough places to sit during the day. He has slept in abandoned buildings, garages, at construction sites, anywhere. Jerry is contemptuous of Children's Aid, but frightened at times by the violence on the street. He has often been terrified by people angry with his punk style of dress. Both the physical beatings and the rejection on the basis of dress anger him.

Yet in spite of all his troubles and his rebellion, Jerry has a gentle spirit, in many ways. He tries never to hold anything against anyone and hopes that, some day, he and his parents will be able to sit down and say to each other, "Hey, how is it going?" He has a hauntingly lovely smile as he explains how hopeless it is for him to look for work with little education and a life on the streets and no home.

It is hard to know what kind of future there will be for this young rebel. Since our interview, I have been looking for him in the drop-ins, but he has melted away into the emptiness of the streets. I am left with the memory of all the unfulfilled promise of his life.

3. Brent: Gifted Misfit/Unemployed Youth

Like Jerry, Brent shatters the stereotype most people have of street people. Exceptionally bright, Brent was clearly a gifted child. Brent's parents are separated and Brent is proud of the achievements of his older brother, who has a good job and has tried to help Brent. Brent finished a course in a field where there are no jobs without a long apprenticeship which he cannot afford. Although Brent managed to stick with school up to two years in college, he was always bored to death in it. School was stagnation, yet Brent's ideas of fun are reading the encyclopedia and playing bridge, scrabble or other competitive intellectual games. He enjoys fellowship at drop-ins and community centres, and the support of others his age on the street who share his interests. Brent has been part of self-help efforts in the past and is currently involved in a new cooperative housing scheme. He says optimistically:

> "I am sure I want to get out of here, but not sure of the best way. I never go with just one scheme, I always have about five on the go."

But Brent also has chilling memories of the past, of being in the psychiatric ward at fourteen, and of a father whose emotional confusion left Brent a shaken child at times. Brent felt that he and his brother helped each other survive their home life. From this model of peer support, Brent has learned to help others on the street and work together on mutual help plans. However, the shadow of his childhoold shows in his insecure self-image: "I do a lot of things in a mediocre way, and a few things well." This statement alternates with others brashly overstating his achievements. Brent is an appealing young man, courteous and eager to help. He is a reflection of the absurdities of a society that allows gifted children to fall through the cracks into the harsh world of the street.

4. Randy, the Mentally Ill on our Streets

Randy looks quite young and is very soft spoken. He sits alone in front of the Scott Mission and looks almost angelic. He lost his job when he left home because he suffered from schizophrenia and has been homeless for seventeen years, off and on. His parents came to Canada from Yugoslavia bringing young Randy. After only four years here, they divorced. He says of them, "They brought me up proper," but there is an apathy and lack of warmth in his voice. Proper upbringing meant a fairly rigid set of expectations that Randy felt he could not meet. He has very little contact with his parents now, seeing his father every two to four years, and his mother only when she visits Canada from France, where she now lives.

School also failed to meet Randy's needs. He found the teaching in school mostly irrelevant to practical survival needs. The main thing that keeps Randy going is an inner voice that helps him "stick with the light." But the struggle for sheer physical survival on the street, getting food and shelter of any kind and keeping modestly clean, is exhausting and depressing to Randy. He feels the poor get caught in a circle, blow their money and get cut off welfare. He has friends who give and receive mutual help from one another, but all of them have emotional ups and downs and it is hard for those caught in a small boat on a stormy sea to steady one another.

Randy wishes there were more free facilities to help him and his friends but he is proud of the progress he has made. Group therapy has helped him gain a stronger grounding. Randy says wistfully, "I want to live the way God wants me to," and one can see his struggle to do just that. He dreams of going back someday to Europe to visit friends there. Randy's survival after seventeen years on the street is a tribute to his stamina and spirit.

5. Rick, Weaver and Rob: A Collage of Native Persons

Three native persons we interviewed illustrate the major paths we see people travelling. Rick is a young native on a dangerous path of alcohol and trauma, heading toward potential violence toward himself or others, and early death. Yet he has a fierce pride in his native heritage and a wistful yearning for a life that will fulfill the promise of that heritage. Weaver is in his mid-thirties and the same kind of start and the same kinds of feelings and dreams have led him to prison, where he now faces long time on a serious charge. Rob is a native who has found his way through these challenges to a path where he can help to build a better life for himself, his family, and other native people.

Rick is just twenty-three. Every member of his family - father, mother, brothers and sisters - is an alcoholic. Rick's father died a violent death when Rick was just sixteen. Rick began taking to the streets then and fell totally into the streets when his mother also died a violent death, leaving him orphaned at nineteen with traumatic memories of the deaths of his parents and with much rage toward the world for their violent deaths.

The brightest spot in Rick's life was a few years in a grade school run by native people which taught awareness of and pride in his native heritage. From this and from his family loyalty come his dreams and, in response to them, he sometimes does volunteer work with native groups. But much of the time he is a loner, brooding over his wrongs and failures. He stole a bike a year ago and while he rode it, felt more linked to the world. But then someone stole it from him and he feels his isolation even more now.

Rick spends winters on the street or, when he is lucky, with a friend who has a room for awhile. Summers are spent entirely on the street.

The freedom of the street is a two-edged sword - Rick enjoys the liberty, but the insecurity and the dangers bother him. From the way average people react to him, Rick feels "like a piece of garbage" on the street. When he lets himself express his inner yearnings, he wishes he could find the sister he has lost touch with and he longs for his dead parents. Lacking life skills, education, work experience, money, and contacts, his chances for a real job are almost nil, and he knows it. He sticks with street friends partly from the terrible fear of being laughed at by others. In many ways, he is still a little boy, craving affection. But he is a child caught in a rough world which will crush him if he cannot find a way through the obstacles which surround him.

Weaver comes from up north. When I first met Weaver, a day when he was just drunk enough to reminisce openly, he moved me deeply by sharing his longing for the woods and the ways of native life up north, and his awareness of how alcohol was destroying him. When we first started the street drop-in where Weaver and I talked, it was Weaver who organized other street people to help us in doing the necessary cleanup.

One day, when Weaver was more drunk than usual and trying to provoke a fight with another drop-in patron, I finally threatened to put him out. Even through his drunken anger, he heard me enough to say, "But I helped build this place." I answered gladly that that was true and we were grateful and would never forget it; and Weaver was detered. Weaver has a sense of humour which often enlivened the drop-in and, despite his dependence on alcohol, his natural talents made him a leader among natives and in the group as a whole.

Weaver's memories of childhood include early memories of his parents bootlegging - alcohol was a curse and a life companion he was born with. His father disappeared when he was young, but his mother and brothers and sisters remain close to him. Most of them have managed to stay off the street. He avoids them now, only because, "I don't want the family to see me tipping the bottle."

We are all getting close to Weaver and beginning to hope he would soon be ready to make a herculean battle with his alcoholism when tragedy struck. A fight broke out on a weekend. The dead body of another native person was found, surrounded by empty bottles of bitters, almost like a pagan rite, symbolizing our worship of this great and destructive god alcohol. Weaver was charged and is currently in custody. His street days are over for the time being and we had a long talk in jail, in which he reminisced about his life. At thirty-three, Weaver still has so much to offer, so many years when he could live. But at this point, his future looks bleak, indeed.

Rob was one of the last people I talked with and my interview with him had a tremendous impact on me. My normal optimism had been gradually sapped by daily immersion in people drowning in life tragedies too big for most of us. I drove, resentfully and wearily, to the other end of town to interview Rob. He and his family were in the cheap motel where metro stores some of the more capable families who overflow the space in our family hostel.

As soon as I walked into the tiny room which housed Rob, his wife, and their three children, I sensed a feeling of light, air, space and above all, peace. It was amazing how this family could transform such limitations into a positive atmosphere. The quiet maturity of Rob's wife, the mannerly behaviour of their children, the beautiful parenting I witnessed, all testified to the fact that this was a remarkable family, who were transcending terible pressures in an inspiring way. Rob himself was tall, well-built, dressed and looked thoroughly native. He oozed radiant good health and good humour and talked like a mature university graduate, although his formal education had ended with high school. When I commented on this, he said, "I have learned that education is an attitude toward life, an attitude of knowing how to go on learning."

Rob's early life began with some all-too familiar patterns. He had an oppressive stepfather who jeered at his achievements and badgered Rob into leaving school in Grade 10, even though Rob was an outstanding student who loved school. Rob left school to get a job to help the family, but also to prove that he could out-drink and out-fight and out-tough his stepfather and all the other native toughs his stepfather held up as models. Rob described his own spiritual evolution as beginning with an internalized view of himself as bad, which came partly from the white school and society teaching him to be ashamed of his race and heritage. His stepfather's influence led him toward the second stage: rage against the outside world, expressed in drinking and fighting. Like most victims of cultural oppression, Rob and his stepfather did their fighting against other victims of oppression, not against the outside oppressors.

The miraculous third step that came next is what separates Rob from most people. Few of us can transcend bounda-

STREET PEOPLE SPEAK

ries and turn "irritation to irridenscence" in the way Rob has. After eight years of hard drinking and fighting, Rob had reached the state where he could outdrink and outfight any of them. He could drink forty beers and some tequilas and still stand; and he could fight any Indian and come out of it well. At this point, he began to question the value of all this.

Rob looked around him and saw the people he hung around with were blubbering idiots after a few hours of drinking. He saw couples fighting and families wasted from it all. He began to get a sense of the uselessness of it all, of the sheer waste of TIME.

Rob could not explain to me totally what the miracle that enabled him to transcend the bonds which few escape. But at this point, he became increasingly clear he wanted to leave behind both hating himself and hating others and to seek to live constructively. He went back to school, deaf to the jeering of his stepfather. He gave up smoking and drinking both, because they "didn't make sense".

Rob finished high school and took training in art. He was constantly advised to go into engineering where he could make a good living, but his sense of direction was more confident all the time and, in spite of all the advice, he was true to his inner call to be a native artist. He and his wife opened their home to all kinds of needy people and expressed their own awarness in helping others. But although Rob and his family are keen to help their people and others in need, at present, their focus is on helping themselves. Rob had evolved by this time far beyond where his original family could understand him - at first his mother would try to trick him into drink. After years of abstaining totally, he has finally reached the point where alcohol has no meaning for him personally, one way or the other. He believes it is important to get way from his former peers, to recognize that he is important, and can make his own decisions. His life is a monumental testimony to his success in doing just that. Rob is working to help other native artists and to build a better world for his children, but also to witness the possibility that a native person can transcend all the barriers and live, as an evolved person, a life bridging creatively his native heritage and modern society.

In this context, the economic troubles which led Rob and his family to migrate across the continent, to move from reserve to city and to find themselves homeless, were just another step in their undefeatable search for a new identity. Rob spoke of their move by bus and all their hardships with a humour that was a part of his incredible maturity. But he spoke feelingly of the factors that have pushed him and most native people into this dilemma:

> "The government wants us to live in the mainstream, but our people say no. We would like to live at home in the wilderness where it still exists, but now there are no animals. You can't even eat two fish a day, and there are no more deer. There is no home left for us. If you do kill a deer, there are worms all over its body; it's disgusting. Our whole people are homeless, and alcoholism is the solvent with which we try to forget."

But Rob's vision goes even beyond his understanding of the tragedy of his people, and his own clear sense of identity and purpose. He cares also about the world and our need to build a world where justice has a central part for all people:

> "The basis of life is sharing. It is sad to see one million eggs go to waste, and one million people starving on the other side. We have to make people realize time is limited, and we have only so many years to learn how to share, to find ourselves and to find the ways in which we can give to the world."

Rick, Weaver and Rob are three lives among the sea of native people made homeless by the clash of our way of life with their native heritage and the failures of our economic and social system. As Rob put it, a whole people are homeless and, as a society, we are not providing adequate answers. The ability of a person with Rob's spiritual gifts to climb the mountain of

STREET PEOPLE SPEAK

A typical scene of homelessness in Toronto's Parkdale area.

Ruth Morris and Colleen Heffren

Home is a park bench in Toronto's Allen Gardens for many street people.

glass does not remove our responsibility to work with native leaders like him in order to provide better answers for all.

6. Dot: Breaking the Pattern of Childhood Abuse

Dot is very articulate. Her words and feelings flow like an open stream. She unabashedly describes how from the age of ten she was shuffled back and forth between her mother's home and a foster home. She is bitter because as a child she was beaten with skipping ropes and army belts. To escape the horror of being molested by her mother's boyfriend and also by her foster father, she left and lived on the streets, "as a tramp". But because she is a sensitive and proud woman, she didn't stay on the streets long.

She met Walt three years before they married and now they have two children, with another one on the way. Despite their own hardships, Walt and Dot are intelligent parents, struggling to give their children the love and security they themselves never had. However, their last apartment was a nightmare experience of landlord harrassment. On New Year's Day they were forced to move upstairs, so the landlord could take over the main floor which they had occupied only one month. Merely walking across the floor, letting the children play, watching T.V., or playing music, evoked screaming reactions about the noise. They became nervous wrecks and, finally, left when the landlord threatened them with a gun and a knife.

Despite their own difficulties, Dot and Walt have provided help to their family. A sister has always sent her children to Dot and Walt for food and a brother lived with them for a while. Because of their compassion, their relatives looked to them as the most stable family members.

Yet Walt, too, has had difficulties, nearly killing himself once with a drug overdose and spending a year on probation for a drug offence. Despite a trade course welfare sent him to, there are no jobs in that field and Walt still struggles with irregular employment. When he gets weekend work, it is hard on Dot to handle the children, particularly since her latest pregnancy.

Dot and Walt struggle to cope with memories of their own traumatic childhoods and want to build a safe and solid life for their own children. In addition, they have joined the increasing ranks of homeless families, struggling merely for a place to live. The lack of affordable housing inhibits them from getting on with their lives and constructively sorting out their emotions about the past. Their children need an environment in which they can grow and become confident citizens in the future society of Canada.

7. Bill: Caught Between Institutions and Street

Bill's current life alternates between summers on the street, winters with travelling carnivals, and institutions which shut him in from these 'freedoms', but at least provide him with an adequate shelter.

Bill's life began on a sordid note with early and repeated experience as a victim of childhood rape. He is obsessed with homosexual rape to the point where one wonders if he is one of those victims who has passed it on by perpetrating it on others. Yet his dreams are about helping kids and especially boys victimized as he was. Right now, he is fighting desperately to learn how to stay out of prison and mental hospitals. Bill spent years in Penetang and has been in six other smaller psychiatric facilities. He is frightened by his own desperate loneliness and would rather be on the street than in a room by himself. He feels a furious anger at the family that failed him and a desperation to escape his institutional-street lose-lose pattern. He is depressed by his many failures, but does not know how to try any harder.

Sometimes, walking around in the early mornings, bumming dollars just for survival and feeling his own overwhelming failure and lack of any future, Bill just cries. He adds, "I wouldn't recommend it for anybody." He feels there are not enough agencies around that really care about truly lost souls like himself. Often, life just becomes mechanical and numbing. His worst feeling is not liking himself. Yet in spite of all his inner and outer troubles, his dreams are to find ways of helping other peole like himself and, above all, of keeping other kids from ending up where he is - thirty-two years old, with no future, no hope, no past to value and a present saturated with despair.

8. Teddy: Caught Between the Rock of Alcohol and the Hard Place of Divorce

Teddy looked so together when I first met him, I wasn't sure whether he was a 'regular' community volunteer, or one of our street people helping out in the drop-in. He turned out to be a durable person with a lot to say for himself, despite five solid years on the street and many years of heavy drinking.

Teddy's story was, in many ways, a fairly common one. He was married, with a wife, a child and a drinking problem. Finally, the drinking problem squeezed the other two out. Like most of the people in this situation, Teddy blamed himself entirely:

"I lost everything through my alcoholic foolishness."

Also like so many others, the divorce pulled out the last prop against his drinking problem, and he then hit bottom. He wasn't always as honest with himself about the cause of it as he is now. At first, he blamed his wife and others and felt a lot of bitterness, particularly over separation from his child, which truly devastated him.

But gradually over the years, not just hitting the bottom, but living on bottom, he began to pull himself together. He went through various alcohol programs, made countless resolutions, broke all of them and through all this gradually learned his own pattern. We all have patterns, be it for drinking, prisons, mental illness, or breaking our diets. Teddy's was a one-month dry maximum pattern. He is aware of it and working hard now to stretch it and, finally, with God's help, to master it. Teddy is thoroughly sick of winters of endless cold and weariness, of rainy days with nowhere to go, of being kicked out of everywhere. Teddy constantly looks for work, and strives to escape his family ghost; his father died of alcoholism at forty-five. He realized his drinking is an effort to "prove I'm no good, and run away from responsibilities." He started drinking at thirteen and has never really stopped.

Teddy's story is one with a happier tint. Since we talked with him, Teddy has gotten off the street for the first time in five years and is making a fresh effort to stay dry, through one of the cooperative homes we are helping them to develop. Teddy's life has a ray of hope just now, but there are so many more Teddys on the streets.

9. Tar: Street Musician

Some people explain away concern for street people by saying that "they choose to live this way". Tar is unique and almost fits this description. He explains his "choice" arises from his mother getting pregnant, his parents' teaching him to think and his refusal to compromise and be controlled. He wants to play music without his creativity being stifled.

Tar is a Grade 13 graduate and has tried working fulltime to pay rent. But he found little time for creativity, so he has been on the street for years. He doesn't take welfare, nor does he use hostels, except in the direst cold. He can't stand the dirt and dangers of hostels, or the unhealthy food.

Tar keeps his independence, but has reasonable, infrequent contacts with his family. He enjoys his freedom, but his sensitive, caring nature draws him into helping a lot of people out of difficulties. A typical day for him includes "meeting about 300 people I know", sketching, and writing.

Tar is aware of our social problems and has deep concerns for world peace. He believes we should "stop living in a dreamland" and that his own uncompromising life is a witness in a small way toward a different society. Tar shared some of his own writings with us:

> "I bought a sketch pad with the money I earned today, and want to play some more to earn supper and a start for tomorrow...
>
> This whole outfit is like the veins on a leaf, all interconnected, smaller and smaller, until a whole multitutde of microscopic universes opens up before your eyes. You look up and see all the leaves on the trees being rustled by the wind...
>
> The reason I am writing this in a storefront on Ann Street is because I got barred from MacDonald's when they did a general cleanup of street people hanging around in the winter to stay warm, and I was included, even though I only drank coffee and read my Bible.
>
> The other donut shops are either too far, or I know too many people who would bug me. At nearest donut shop, I used the bathroom twice already, so I don't want to abuse my privileges. And the park is cold and windy still.
>
> ...I was told to go home before I woke up today, beside a back alley parking lot grassy area, all wrapped up nice and warm in my blankets and plastic, because though it threatened to pour acid rain, it only showered a bit.
>
> I looked up and saw a woman in uniform. A quick check of the stripe up the pant leg (red) and I knew it was no security guard. Her partner asked her who I was and she said, "The guy who plays the guitar on the corner."
>
> I said, 'give me twenty minutes to pack up my gear...'
>
> ... Soon some guy who is finishing off the last two days of a restaurant job bums a smoke and sits down. I tell him my story and he reacts appropriately. I knew him off Queen Street, when he used to send shrinks off on a loop,

telling them about the colours in his head; and slept in an abandoned chicken coop in the market...

A lady threw me a Christian pamplet about Palsm 22. You know the one, the one that starts:

'My God, My God, Why hast thou forsaken me?' Chirst's line as he hung on the cross.

Happy Easter and it's after midnight. I've been writing about yesterday. It is finished.

Tomorrow is another day."

10. David, Older Alcoholic

David is included here to remind us of the many older men we met on the streets, although he is not typical of all. Many of them have no drinking problem. After a lifetime of work and contribution to our society, they are simply castaways with inadequate income and family supports in their old age. David does have a drinking problem and has exacerbated his situation by it, but he is by no means a heavy alcoholic. At sixty-two, he might be looking forward to a happy retirement with lots of hobbies and friends. Instead, he finds himself on the streets.

David began shouldering responsibilities when he left school in Grade 8 to help support the family. He worked solidly for thirty-four years as a truck driver and did a stint in the army, as well. He sometimes does volunteer work now as he likes being busy and meeting people. He is by no means a shirker. But since his wife divorced him, partly for his drinking, his health has also been going downhill, preventing him from working at the heavy jobs he has done in the past. He is not sure which he misses most: his wife, his home, or his work. Looming above all is his deteriorating health. He has five major health problems, but through it all, he goes on quietly trying to help others through volunteer work and remembering those worse off than himself. Despite his poor health, he sometimes spends winter nights in abandoned cars on the street. David is one of our many lonely senior castoffs.

11. Andre and Diane: Job Loss Makes a Family Homeless

Andre's story was told briefly in the "Slide into the Street". One of the most important messages of this book is that there are many Andre's, people who have fallen from established middle class positions, by life accidents, into the shock of homelessness. Andre's story is particularly moving because his fall coincided with the birth of his first child, andthe cry of his homeless baby haunts us with all its symbolism and all of its stark reality.

Andre was an immigrant worker who came to Canada about fifteen years ago. After several years of working hard at two poor paying jobs in order to establish himself, and following all the proper steps that those who want to get ahead in this world are advised to do, Andre got a good paying job at $15 an hour as a skilled machinist. But the work was stressful and demanding. The constantly changing shifts were hard on health and safety and few people lasted as long as Andre did, nine years. After he lost his temper and hit his supervisor under provocation, he, of course, lost his job. Even though that was a year and a half ago, it is hard for Andre not to brood about it. He has not had a decent job since. Automation is cutting jobs in his field and he must look for a new occupation, just when family needs make it hard for him to consider seeking new training. He agonizes again and again over the loss of temper that cost him his job, yet he occasionally wonders wistfully why, after so many years of steady hard work, life couldn't have allowed him one mistake without charging him such a horrendous, unending toll.

The months that should have been glad months for the couple, of anticipating and planning the birth of their first child, saw instead the gradual seeping away of unemployment insurance, leading to welfare and finally to no affordable housing. Andre is so eager to prove to me how hard he is trying, but he doesn't need to prove it to me: it permeates everything he does, from his eagerness to give something to the world through this interview to his excellent phone manner in talking to a prospective landlady. He is amazed that this could have happened to him and he has a desire to tell the world so we can all understand, so that his family's suffering may not be wholly in vain.

Most touching is Andre's devotion to his wife and baby. The one positive thing he can see in the situation is how close he has been able to be with his baby daughter, whom he calls by an affectionate nickname. Andre describes warmly the kindness of strangers and laments the failures of some family and friends. He admits it is harder for him to receive from family what little they have offered: "I can't help resenting them because they are so comfortably off, and our position is so bad."

One can't help wondering, looking at Andre's dark skin, how far race prejudice has aggravated his job and home search, given the recent research documenting extensive race discrimination in certain areas of Toronto. But Andre never murmurs about this. He just wants to get on with his life, to redouble his own efforts to find housing and employment to re-establish his family. He does feel it is harder at his age - near forty - to start over; and he continues to soul search both for new ways of beating the system successfully and answers to the ancient "Why me?" dilemma.

Andre and Diane are no crybabies. In their crowded room, struggling with the humiliation of their situation, they express joy at the wonder of their baby and appreciation for their welfare worker and others who have helped them. The question is, what are we doing to create enough affordable housing for families like theirs?

CHAPTER SEVEN:
COMMUNITY ACTION

After the experiences of meeting so many homeless people, it is impossible to ignore the huge injustice of their plight. It is also hard not to be alarmed by this socially destablilizing trend which is sweeping across our country and the world. The requirement of communities to concern themselves actively with government housing policies is essential to turn this crisis around. The practice of locking people out of housing that is economically inaccessible, board-up, slated for demolition, or conversion to luxury condominiums can no longer be tolerated. Our society has displaced the value of human life with the "value" of housing as a commodity. These policies reinforce the denial of people's basic right to housing. Thus we need to begin from the premise of honouring the right of all people to decent and affordable housing. The United

Nations consider the homeless to include both the unsheltered street people, as well as those who endure substandard living accommodation. Housing therefore, by the U.N. definition, should provide adequate protection from the elements; access to safe water and sanitation; secure tenure and personal safety; and accessibility to employment, education and health care services.

We need to ensure that government policies honour this basic requirement of housing people and uphold the value of human life to protect the stability of our society. A starting point would be to allocate all public funds for housing to the non-profit and co-op housing sector. Complementary initiatives would also be a government commitment to make affordable housing units available by building new units and, also, accessing the many vacant properties presently left dormant in our cities. The Affordable Housing Action Group recommends for Ontario a commitment to 120,000 units over a five year period. By implementing these goals, we can put into practice people's basic right to affordable housing.

The crisis of homelessness is with us now and concrete government planning is essential to avert the inevitable tragic escalation of more middle-to-low income people landing in the streets. Lack of government planning has led to the loss of affordable housing largely due to the gentrification process of demolishing, converting, renovating or upgrading housing. It is estimated that in the City of Toronto alone, an average of five affordable units are lost each day, with the building of two, for a net daily loss of three units. In the U.S., developers who demolish or convert affordable housing stock must pay into a fund to replenish affordable housing. Legislation should be passed which will protect the affordable housing stock from gentrification and support the renovation and up-grading of vacant housing for low-income people.

Political initiatives to institute more hostels to remedy the glaring lack of affordable housing will only aggravate an unbearable situation. Hostels are not designed to support, comfort, nor empower people to regain control over their lives.

STREET PEOPLE SPEAK

Instead, they tend to perpetuate the social assistance revolving door syndrom which keeps the homeless on the streets. Hostels are needed for temporary emergency shelter for the very "hard to house" and also for families and individuals unexpectedly struck with tragedy. Hostels cannot replace the need of people for independent housing which gives them the opportunity of building their lives with dignity. Only permanent and affordable housing can enable people to look after themselves and become restored participants in society.

In addition to the lack of affordable housing, housing the homeless necessitates offering essential human resources to resond to the severity of emotional and personal disarray which the homeless suffer. Our welfare system is designed to provide only a bureaucratic service of processing welfare claims. Caring welfare workers are not able to offer the daily contact and counselling services which are often necessary in the initial stabilizing period of housing the homeless. Services for the homeless are often passed from one office to another, with the client breaking down before being able to access any support. This only defeats and embitters the homeless when they are trapped, locked-out or unable to access sufficient funds for rent, health care, appropriate work clothing, etc. More co-ordination of services is essential to protect those who fall through the social safety net to support their survival efforts.

Healing the trauma which poverty and homelessness perpetuate requires implementing support services which recognize and respond to the desperate personal needs of the homeless. As labelled members of our community, the homeless are discriminated against and they are frequently unable to overcome the barriers to find safe and affordable housing. Psychiatric patients are released into our communities without suitable housing and sufficient support services. Facilities to protect and support the healing needs of ex-psychiatric patients are essential. Similarly, ex-prisoners do not have the social coping skills to support their integration into the community. Fear, isolation and frustration only feed their self-destructive attitudes. Abused women and children need safe and stable environments to rebuild their lives. More facilities are needed to provide transitional housing and independent living arrangements for people moving out of institutions. In order to remedy the immense isolation of the homeless, many more community workers are needed to set the homeless up with counselling, training, medical care and, most important of all, affordable housing. A registry of housing is essential in each community which would be co-ordinated through a facilitator who can support the differing needs of the various groups. A registry alone is inadequate as people need to be guided into a suitable situation and supported in the process of reclaiming their independence.

Challenging the economic factors perpetuating poverty, especially as they impact on children, is essential to arrest the burgeoning social disease of homelessness. Poverty is a decisive factor in the slide to the streets. The unemployed, the working poor and shelter recipients spend sixty to seventy percent of their income on shelter.[1] Little remains for food, transportation, clothing or personal necessities, let alone any unexpected expenses. A social safety net must protect the poor from homelessness. Raising the minimum wage to ensure a standard of living above the poverty level is one step. A system of rental assistance should be available to protect the housing of low-income people. Work in the home is often essential for families raising children, caring for the elderly, or those with disabilities. This is unrecognized labour, but it should be valued and supported financially by society as a whole. These policies must be implemented as a part of a comprehensive government program to protect the living standards of all Canadians.

The need to secure a social safety net is abundantly clear, especially when considering the economic strains on families raising children. Child poverty increased twenty-three percent in Canada between 1980 and 1985.[2]

Systemic poverty, which discourages families from raising children, is reinforced by the lack of affordable housing, unemployment, inadequate income and insufficient day care spaces.

The rising number of sole support mothers also contributes to the increase in child poverty, as women only earn two-thirds the salaries of men. The increasing reality of child poverty is a disgrace which will undermine the best efforts of government, community and industry to rectify this social injustice. The Child Poverty Action Group (CPAG) have pin-pointed a practical and preventive planning policy which the federal government should implement to ensure equal chances for all children. A Universal Child Income Credit (UCIC) is proposed in which parents would receive $3,600 a year for the first child and $3,000 a year for each subsequent child. This amount is based on the average cost of raising a child in Metro Toronto. Parents may choose to receive the benefit as either a 'cash credit', through monthly advance payments, or as a 'tax credit', through the income tax return. The second proposal is a Parental Employment Income Guarantee (PEIG), which (1) compensates for the absence of adequate and suitable employment for parents and (2) gives parents a choice whether or not they want to play a more active parenting role at critical stages of their child's development. The PEIG should be about $13,200, or sixty percent of the average industrial wage. This amount, combined with the UCIC, would guarantee an adequate social floor of income for families with children.[3]

More and more youths are finding themselves locked in the syndrome of street life. They are runaway kids who are emotionally confused. Often, they have been abused, or their families, unable to cope, throw them out. Huge efforts are needed to establish drop-in centres for youths and

children which offer safe and supportive environments. Programs should be developed which will integrate the input and interests of young people, to keep them off the streets. Support programs should include literacy classes; life skills; peer counselling; self-development; job training; health care, etc.

Homelessness, itself, carries an overpowering social stigma which prevents many young people from landing full time employment. Few employers are willing to hire anyone who does not have an address, or who lives in a hostel. This stigma, combined with the emotional despair which the down and out experience, keeps them from helping themselves. Community employment referral centres should be established to liaise with appropriate government and business offices to develop more appropriate employment opportunities for the homeless. This service could also link up the needs for skills training, education upgrading, counsellling and employment referrals in a comprehensive approach.

This overview of community action is not intended to be a rigorous analysis for the various housing advocacy proposals. Rather, we have simply provided a framework of some pertinent issues which reflect our concerns. For a more in depth portrayal of the ideas discussed here, we encourage further reference to the following resources and organizations:

An Agenda For Action: The Nine Point Program, The Affordable Housing Action group, c/o The Social Planning Council of Metro, Toronto, August, 1987.

Canadian Housing, The Canadian Association of Housing and Renewal Officials, May 15, 1986, Vol.3, No.2, and March 31, 1987, Vol.4, No.1.

A Place to Call Home, Housing Solutions for Low-Income Singles in Ontario, Report of the Ontario Task Force on Roomers, Boarders and Lodgers to the Honourable Alvin Curling, Minister of Housing, December, 1986.

FOOTNOTES

1. *Social Development Overview,* Canadian Council on Social Development, Vol.4, No.1, 1986; and Vol.4, No.3, Summer 1987, 55 Parkdale, Box 3505, Station C, Ottawa, K1Y 4G1.

2. *The National Income Program for Children, Policies to End Child Poverty*, Child Poverty Action Group, 1987, 950 Yonge Street, Suite 1000, Torotno, M4Z 2J4.

3. Ibid.

CONCLUSION

This book has exposed the unreality of life on the streets, by empowering the voices of the unknown and silent street people in our midst. By understanding the moving plight of the homeless, we can become more sensitized to the needs of being human and, in turn, work to redress the crushing systemic conditions which are cited as the primary causes of homelessness. While we have not addressed the economic conditions of low income, unemployment and the lack of affordable housing in their entirety, these factors, indeed, perpetrate wide-spread homelessness. Our extensive caring service system cannot rectify this problem.

The most striking fact about the homeless is that not one single cause or problem contributes to their being locked into this situation. People suffer from a multitude of problems ranging from poverty, health, family breakdown, psychiatric, personal trauma, alcohol, illiteracy, etc. But, often, homelessness is the initial cause of these problems; homelessness <u>itself</u> is a primary problem afflicting the strong and weak alike. Once they are caught in the net of institutionalization and are labelled by society, street people themselves are forced to wear their labels poorly for fear of losing even this limited and impersonal support.

One feels a special grief for young people, whose lives are lost in the tangle of homelessness, hopelessness and treatment of institutionalization. Yet the young are compassionate and movingly concerned for those worse off them themselves. The growing legacy of homelessness is endured silently by the unlucky and the poor. We classify street people as bums or derelicts which separates "us" from "them". This helps us forget that they are needy human beings, just like us. When we ignore the plight of such stark human need, people who are hungry for understanding and acceptance, the impact of homelessness on our communities can only dehumanize us. But not all street people are pitiful victims of multi-generational poverty. No one is safe, as we witness the "new group of refugees" who have fallen from the middle class onto the streets thorugh the trauma of high unemployment, family breakup, etc.

The real "Catch 22" for many people is not being able to get a job because they don't have an address; and not being able to get first and last month's rent together because they don't have a job. Even though social assistance will provide first and last month's rent with the promise of an address, few landlords will take in anyone on assistance. So great is the stigma against welfare. People in this position are also fully aware that they are up against a judgmental system. The pain and humiliation of being dissected by social services forces people back to the seeming privacy of the streets. Or, it forces them to wear their labels of emotional and/or physical disability in a self-defeating way.

STREET PEOPLE SPEAK

The homeless wage an enormous battle to survive. But once reduced to this bare existence, their health rapidly deteriorates. Many diseases including ringworm and tuberculosis assail the unsheltered. The task of housing and empowering the poor to regain their dignity and self-respect is a fundamental imperative for our society.

Cold concrete steps of churches in Toronto are often the only places left to catch a night's rest.

Ruth Morris and Colleen Heffren

End of a day for Toronto's poor who haven't found work and have no place to go with nothing to do.

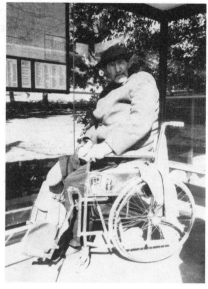

APPENDIX ON METHODOLGY

It was decided to interview fifty to one hundred street people for this book and the issue of sampling was carefully considered. There was no way of careful sampling from a known pool of the total street people. Consequently, we made sure that we interviewed people in a wide variety of settings: in different drop-ins, agencies and on the street itself, in various parts of town. In the absence of a random sample, we made sure our sample included significant numbers from the following categories:

both sexes
all ages
native people and blacks
longer and shorter time street people
homeless families as well as individuals

Ruth Morris and Colleen Heffren

We hired one interviewer who spoke Ojibway and had extensive experience with native people to supplement out interviewing with native people.

In the end, eight-two interviews were obtained, although these varied greatly in quality. We found that the longer a person had been on the street, the more the experience debilitated his or her capacity to give a "normal" interview with full articulation of one's views. Therefore, many of the interviews with those longest on the street gave us more of a tone of response than words to quote. Fortunately, a few of the long-termers and many of the short-termers were extremely articulate and we have tried to include the feelings of the others in our commentary.

People who least expect to find themselves on the streets, who have had homes and jobs, settle in front of the Church of the Redeemer hoping to find answers or at least some support at Avenue Rd. and Bloor in Toronto.